FROM NARROW-BLINDED
— TO —
OPEN MINDED

An Alternative Approach for
Improved Decision-Making

EDWARD N. GAMBLE, PHD, CPA

This publication is designed to provide accurate and authoritative information in regard to the subject matter covered. It is sold with the understanding that the publisher and author are not engaged in rendering legal, accounting, or other professional services. Nothing herein shall create an attorney-client relationship, and nothing herein shall constitute legal advice or a solicitation to offer legal advice. If legal advice or other expert assistance is required, the services of a competent professional should be sought.

Published by River Grove Books
Austin, TX
www.rivergrovebooks.com

Copyright © 2024 Ogham Consulting Group LLC
All rights reserved.

Thank you for purchasing an authorized edition of this book and for complying with copyright law. No part of this book may be reproduced, stored in a retrieval system, or transmitted by any means, electronic, mechanical, photocopying, recording, or otherwise, without written permission from the copyright holder.

Distributed by River Grove Books

Design and composition by Greenleaf Book Group and Sheila Parr
Cover design by Greenleaf Book Group and Sheila Parr
Interior illustrations were commissioned for this book by the author and illustrated by Soufyane Zanfoukh.

Publisher's Cataloging-in-Publication data is available.

Print ISBN: 978-1-63299-859-0

eBook ISBN: 978-1-63299-860-6

First Edition

Praise for *From Narrow-Blinded to Open Minded*

"Edward Gamble's *From Narrow-Blinded to Open Minded* is an extraordinary book on contempt—a key problem in our culture. It offers a hopeful message: By recognizing our biases, and being open to new ideas, we can reverse course and grow better, together."

—**Arthur C. Brooks,** professor, Harvard Kennedy School and Harvard Business School and #1 *New York Times* best-selling author

"In this inspiring new book, Edward Gamble's penetrating analysis enables the reader to harness the opportunities accruing from being open minded rather than succumbing as a victim to the narrow-minded. The book is a delightful fusion of rock-solid scholarship and science combined with literary agility and a touch of self-help. The result is a mesmerizing bouquet of insights with the promise for self-transformation, liberation, and enlightenment."

—**David Audretsch,** distinguished professor, Ameritech Chair of Economic Development, and director, Institute for Development Strategies, Paul H. O'Neill School of Public and Environmental Affairs, University of Indiana

"This provocative book is like a road trip with a wise, witty friend. Your thinking will become more evidence-based and discerning along the way."

—**Denise M. Rousseau,** H.J. Heinz II University Professor of Organizational Behavior and Public Policy; director, Project on Evidence-Based Organizational Practices; Heinz College and Tepper School of Business, Carnegie Mellon University

"Gamble's 3T model—think, talk about it, and take action—provides an engaging framework for breaking free from the constraints of polarization, which are increasingly prevalent in our universities and communities. By encouraging a holistic view and fostering open-minded dialogue, Gamble empowers readers to navigate complex challenges with clarity and creativity. This book is an essential read for anyone committed to embracing alternative perspectives, enhancing their problem-solving capabilities, and driving meaningful change in both personal and professional spheres."

—**Matthew Grimes,** director, MPhil in Innovation, Strategy, and Organisation Programme; codirector, The Entrepreneurship Centre; and professor, Entrepreneurship and Sustainable Futures, Judge Business School; University of Cambridge

"Dr. Gamble's superpower is his ability to see complex issues clearly by avoiding the common pitfalls of groupthink, cognitive bias, and overconfidence. He shares with us his powerful approach to thinking so that we may become more effective in our careers and in our personal relationships."

—**Doug Fletcher,** best-selling author of *How Clients Buy* and *How To Win Client Business*

"Edward Gamble weaves together a wonderful tapestry of science and storytelling. A habitual world traveler, Gamble draws on his experiences to highlight the importance of shaking off our blinders and embracing the world around us. He shares his learning journey with enthusiasm and joy, inviting all of us to think, discuss, and act together."

—**Stewart Thornhill,** executive director, Zell Lurie Institute for Entrepreneurial Studies; Eugene Applebaum Professor of Entrepreneurial Studies; Ross School of Business, University of Michigan

I am eternally grateful to my close friends for the joy and laughter they bring into my life!

Contents

Preface ix
Introduction: I'm Right and You're Wrong 1

THINK! 15
1: The Illusion of Knowledge 17
2: "Fake News" . . . and My Truth 37
3: Getting in Touch with Your Inner Yoda 53

TALK ABOUT IT! 67
4: Group Blinders 69
5: Shaking Off Overconfidence 85
6: The Power of Effective Explanation 99

TAKE ACTION! 117
7: Small Steps, Giant Leaps: Exploring Small-Scale Experiments . . 119
8: Improvement Doesn't Happen by Chance 135
9: From Idea to Action: The Effectuation Way 151

CONCLUSION
Brace for Impact 167
Acknowledgments 177
Notes 179
About the Author 185

Preface

IN VARIOUS CHAPTERS OF MY LIFE, I have stumbled upon moments of internal calmness—a rare ceasefire in the battles with my own restlessness. My close friends would probably say that quelling the Edward fervor is not easy. Yet, in the occasional moments of serenity, stillness becomes indelible. As a child, the narrow, stonewalled country roads of Ireland served as the setting for these tranquil interludes. Traveling with my family, we would wind through the country roads and villages, pausing for the simple pleasure of a chocolate flake in an ice cream cone. Many of these roads were shrouded by overarching trees, bordered by stone walls, and punctuated by bends and twists that cast an enthralling spell. The tight confines, often concealed by overgrown ivy, barely allowed space for two passing cars, and created an atmosphere of peaceful seclusion. Even the occasional encounter with a herd of cattle or sheep ambling down the road added to the tranquility.

Years have passed since I traveled the rural Irish roads, yet similar moments of mental quietude often revisit me. Exiting the mountain pass from Big Sky to Bozeman, Montana, after a day of skiing, brings the same effect. The half-frozen, swift-moving river on the right and the imposing mountains surrounding the pass evoke a sense of serenity. Steinbeck's sentiment about Montana resonates deeply: "I am in love with Montana. For other states I have admiration, respect, recognition, even some affection, but with Montana it is love, and it's difficult to analyze love when you're in it."[1] More recently, the drive through Shelburne Farms in Vermont, with its sprawling working farm, gravel roads, panoramic views of Lake Champlain, native wildflowers, and the distant Adirondack Mountains, recreated that feeling.

What binds these diverse experiences? Many of my moments of calmness, peace, and perhaps my clearest thinking have occurred on winding rural roads. From the Tongariro Crossing in New Zealand to the villages, onsens, and Buddhist temples along the tiny roads of Kyushu, Japan, each experience stands in stark contrast to the chaos of the US interstates or the Trans-Canada highway. The cluttered and frenzied rush of these major highways leaves me feeling lost, my head spinning like Beetlejuice. The constant rush to move from one point to the next as swiftly as possible led by the perpetual go-go-go type of person who is driven by an incessant urge to be in constant motion renders me breathless. High speeds, tired transport truck drivers mere feet away, and ubiquitous bumper-to-bumper traffic create a maddening sense of being herded, akin to cattle.

Oddly, conventional wisdom upholds the highway as the superior route for travel. It seems to be universal and absolute. But why? Major highways, much like our prevailing modes of thinking and decision-making, are assumed to be the best path, causing us to overlook alternative routes. It's a blind spot we seem to have developed collectively. Any deviation from the dominant view—the major highway route—is quickly judged to be naïve, foolish, or simply ridiculous.

Most would argue that they take highways because it offers the most direct route, as reaching a destination swiftly is the only priority. This illustrates our prevailing logic—we seek the most direct route of thinking because it propels us to a conclusion as expeditiously as possible. But what insights might we glean from exploring alternative routes?

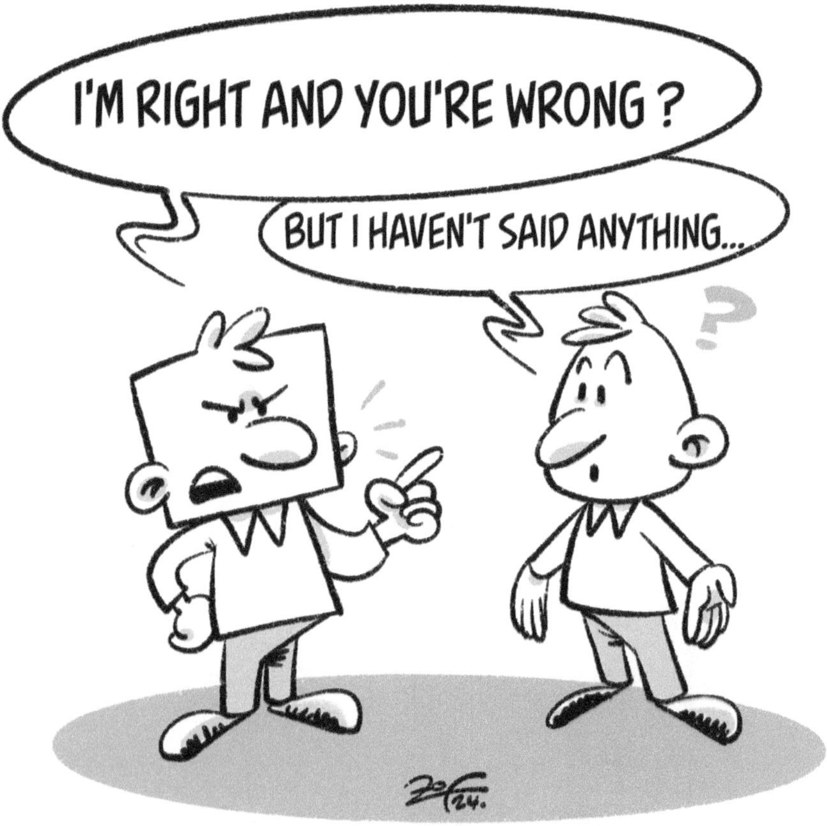
I'M RIGHT AND YOU'RE WRONG ?
BUT I HAVEN'T SAID ANYTHING...

Introduction

I'm Right and You're Wrong

"Hatred is an affair of the heart; contempt is that of the head."
—Arthur Schopenhauer

Narrow-Blindedness

In the montage of my Irish experience, from growing up in an Irish Catholic family to summers with family in Ireland, workdays in Cork, and academic pursuits in Dublin, I've come to understand that growing up in an Irish milieu is akin to mastering a unique set of cultural codes. Undoubtedly, this holds true not only for Irish immigrants in Canada but also for those who have traversed the Atlantic to the United States or ventured down under to Australia.

Irrespective of the geographical setting, a consistent thread weaves through the fabric of Irish identity—the art of disagreeing with wit. The skill is not so much rooted in malice but in a playful sharpness that suggests one might be missing something in their thinking. The ability to engage in quick-witted banter is as ingrained in the Irish psyche as the love for Barry's tea, the graceful insertion of swear words mid-conversation, the peculiar practice of unmarried couples sleeping in separate rooms when visiting parents, the sheer delight in England's defeats in any sporting event, the fervor for hurling (coupled with its inherent violence), the devotion to Taytos and full Irish breakfasts, the pursuit of craic and good-natured slagging, and the fortitude of names with complex pronunciations that leave others flummoxed. In essence, discussion, debate, and disagreement are not just conversational tools in Ireland; they are integral to the Irish way of thinking.

It wasn't until later in life that the true value and wisdom of this constant, thoughtful construction of arguments and the ensuing healthy discussion and debate in the Irish psyche became apparent to me. For some reason I am envisioning a spirited discourse between two old Irish men in a pub right now, puffing on their pipes, passionately debating modern politics and economics.

A fundamental and enduring benefit of this social acceptance of open discussion, debate, and disagreement in Ireland is the fortification against what I term "narrow-blindness." Throughout this book, you'll frequently encounter this phrase, so let me provide some context. The term "narrow" by itself isn't inherently negative; a narrow or hyper-focused approach often leads to virtuosity in various fields, as evidenced by historical figures like Bach, Mozart, Rembrandt, Michelangelo, and da Vinci. However, when applied to the task of understanding multifaceted matters, an excessively narrow approach can result in severe blindness—a blindness that causes one to miss opportunities. This myopic perspective, which is generally absolute or extreme, hinders perception and judgment, putting the perceiver in a position akin to a hippo traversing a tightrope over a field of nails in pitch-black darkness. It is a perilous and costly endeavor!

Narrow-blindedness, as I see it, distinguishes itself from the more common term "narrow-mindedness." The latter involves an unwillingness to accept anything unusual or different. However, in my experience, the core of our human disposition lies in our innate eagerness and willingness to draw as close to "the truth" as possible. Fundamentally, I believe we desire knowledge, and most individuals are open to embracing the unusual or different if it propels us toward a deeper understanding of truth. The difficulty often lies in the lack of a proper toolset or approach to navigate alternative routes. Instead of refining our approaches or toolsets to better manage the barrage of information we receive, we find ourselves paralyzed and often in confrontation with alternative views.

I characterize the term "narrow-blindedness" as the act of forgoing the opportunity to see something unexpected by becoming "lost" in our preexisting perspectives. The analogy extends seamlessly into our daily thinking and logic, a concept I've observed and ruminated on for well over a decade.

The root of this tension, in my estimation, stems from an ingrained false belief that we must exude supreme confidence in being "right" in our assessments, and that those who disagree with us must be unequivocally wrong. To explore this dynamic, I've embarked on a decade-long social experiment; a form of ethnography, I suppose. The ongoing experiment has been a fascinating exploration. Although, I must admit my wife has caught on to my endeavors, prompting a notice that my line of questioning is off-limits at family events.

A Tipping Point

My fascination with the concept of narrow-blindedness traces back to a convivial gathering of close friends, a genial bunch who possess remarkable senses of humor and do not take themselves too seriously. This eclectic group, with backgrounds spanning engineering, mining, business, science, military defense, and education, never fails to spark thought-provoking conversations. It all began over cocktails with a question that resonates deeply: If you could instantly solve one problem facing humanity, what would it be? So, dear reader, take a moment to set this book aside (but not for too long—we have much ground to cover) and ponder your answer, perhaps envisioning the type of beverage you'd be sipping while thinking about this question. For the record, I was enjoying my favorite—an old-fashioned.

Some might suggest global food security, living wages, human rights, economic poverty, or political governance—all valid perspectives in my mind. But what if a singular, targeted solution could simultaneously impact and maybe even solve multiple challenges? How would we measure such an impact? The cocktail-fueled query got me contemplating the greatest advances in human civilization and the barriers or costs that accompanied such progress. Given my background in accounting and tax, I habitually ponder the costs of our choices.

As I sat engrossed in the insightful responses from people I deeply admire, my good friend Doug, author of two best-selling books, put the spotlight on me, asking what I thought. I responded, "Contempt is the biggest problem facing society."

Cue a smirk from Doug, followed by, "Typical Ed answer. What do you mean by that?"

My train of thought at that moment was humanity's inability to veer away from firmly held beliefs to move toward compromise, and that such unwillingness to see an alternative route is the paramount challenge of our time. We spend considerable time committed to a specific stance or direction (potentially spouting nonsense to justify it) because we lack the tools to pause and consider a course correction—an alternative route. Using half-baked logic, we delude ourselves into believing our direction is unequivocally correct, prompting us to dismiss divergent views as worthless.[1] Take a look at modern political discourse—a breeding ground for contempt, where each side sees their views as benevolent and the opposing side as rooted in nonsense, with a dash of evil. This does little to solve grand problems and squanders valuable opportunities for positive change.

Contempt, in simple terms, is the belief that we are categorically right, and those who disagree are categorically wrong and perhaps daft for not seeing it our way. Social psychologist Jonathan Haidt links contempt to the enjoyment people derive from scandals—both provide a sense of moral superiority.[2] It's almost like pointing out others' failings helps us bond over shared ground and overlook our own hypocrisy.

Unfortunately, many have not taken heed to the insights of Buddha, who so wisely proclaimed, "It is easy to see the faults of others, but difficult to see one's own faults."

Contempt isn't an anomaly; it's pervasive. It crept into 1980s sitcoms and has firmly embedded itself in our social media accounts. Algorithms in our daily lives fuel this fire, encouraging us to feel contemptuous and morally superior. Social media and news outlets capitalize on these emotions to keep us coming back for more, fostering shock, polarization, and, you guessed it, contempt. Kudos to the marketeers for fueling the contempt train!

Fixing everything by waving a wand and saying, "No more contempt!" would be nice, but that is perhaps unrealistic. So, what's a workable solution? I propose a toolbox, or rather an approach to identify fractures in logic and strategies for course correction—better ways of thinking, talking about ideas, and taking action. Contempt, after all, is the byproduct of sloppy thinking, reluctance to share perspectives, and a lack of proactive measures to course correct. Therefore, at the heart of this book is a mission to extinguish what I term narrow-blinded thinking; and in doing so I hope that we can dial down the associated contempt levels. It's time for a more thoughtful journey. All aboard!

Unraveling the Costs of Narrow-Blindedness

The crux of the matter is, hastily branding something as categorically wrong, without giving it careful consideration, can lead to significant costs. Pause for a moment and reflect on the harm or hurt you've seen stemming from mislabeling and misjudgments in relationships, business dealings, public policy, and contempt in key leadership roles. Chances are, you can recall at least one instance and the associated costs.

Having seen much of the world over the course of many years, I've witnessed the profound costs of narrow-blindedness and the extensive negative impact of its fallout, comparable in size and scale to a global pandemic. Hence, the thesis of this book is: Narrow-blindedness is toxic. It fosters poor decision-making and results in dreadful and costly outcomes on multiple levels.

Think back to those uncomfortable moments you've had with family members, friends, or colleagues, as one of them regaled you with their absolutist perspective. It's as if they were delivering a theatrical monologue, leaving you in a bewildered silence, trying to politely hide your pained expression. The air was quickly sucked out of the room, prompting feeble attempts to shift the discourse to mundane subjects such as the day's weather, because rarely does anyone summon the courage to unravel the tightly wrapped package of biased views presented before them.

The canvas of this scene is painted with the hues of rigid opinions, the brushstrokes of awkward silences, and the splashes of attempts to redirect the conversation. Instead of giving space to a wide palette of diverse ideas, this scene is stifled by the dull shades of narrow-blindedness.

Many of us have witnessed firsthand what happens when contentious topics, such as current politics, government regulation, tax policy, or environmental planning, are injected into a conversation. These exchanges become intensely charged and typically unfold in a predictable, confrontational fashion. They resemble a well-rehearsed theatrical performance of "I'm right and you're wrong." Picture the setting: a conversational stage where the spotlight hones in on a spicy topic, introduced with a metaphorical drumroll. Enter the protagonist, a strong-minded and vocal individual who fearlessly wades into the murky waters of dialogue ready to put on a carefully crafted performance. Their act—a concoction of pseudo-evidence, an abundance of (over)confidence, and skillfully woven rhetoric—sets the stage for what is about to unfold.

As this charismatic orator passionately presents their perspective, the audience has a spectrum of reactions. Some, perhaps out of fear, a desire to avoid awkwardness, or the inclination toward pseudo-agreement, nod in apparent support. It's a silent ballet of conformity as much of the audience is cowed by this forceful performance.

However, just when the atmosphere seems saturated with consensus, there comes a disruptive chord. Someone in the crowd, with furrowed eyebrows, offers a response laced with hostility followed by a barrage of heated counterarguments. The bottle comes uncorked. In that moment, the dormant tension erupts into a full-fledged confrontation. Contempt, now revved up on both sides, permeates the air like an electric charge of intolerance, crackling with the anticipation of verbal combat.

Let the games begin. The stage transforms into an arena of gladiators, each armed with their arsenal of beliefs and convictions. The conversation, once a calm and respectful sea, is now a tempest of conflicting ideas, where the clash of opinions rings like thunder and the waters roil with high waves of impassioned discourse and mean-spirited words.

In these instances, does anyone's opinion truly change? Probably not. In fact, entrenched views don't merely stand their ground; they fortify themselves, becoming even more impervious. Conversations clouded by contempt make it even less likely that we'll consider alternative routes.

The Rot in the Logic-Carcass Is All Around Us

A sizable reduction of narrow-blinded thinking, absolutism, and contempt emerges as a key first step in the broader quest to improve our lives; as well as the broader efforts to alleviate poverty and hunger, enhance health and well-being, provide superior education and clean water, refine energy policies, increase employment, and spur economic growth. It underpins and encompasses comprehensive reforms in industry, education, and infrastructure, the development of sustainable cities, the cultivation of responsible consumption practices, conflict reduction, and initiatives for positive transformations in climate, water, and land ecosystems—take your pick.

The nefarious and hidden toll of narrow-blinded thinking manifests in a plethora of detrimental ways. Take a moment to think about how narrow-blinded thinking has impacted your life, business, and/or community. Remember what A.A. Milne wrote in his book *Winnie-the-Pooh*: "Did you ever stop to think, and forget to start again?" From time to time, I am guilty as charged. When delving into complex topics like the costs of narrow-blinded thinking, it's all too easy to lose one's way and forget to consider the grave costs. Here are a few examples, or rather reflections, on the layers and costs associated with narrow-blindedness. These might motivate us on our journey.

1. Cultivating and nurturing meaningful connections is paramount to fostering healthy relationships in all areas of our lives. The costs of adopting a narrow-blinded approach to these connections can be far-reaching, affecting not only our relationships with spouses, friends, children, and spiritual communities, but also contributing to broader societal issues. The detrimental consequences of harboring contemptuous attitudes become glaringly apparent in the alarming rise of divorce rates, heightened family conflicts, and the surge of religious fanaticism. By having a set of tools that guides a more expansive and open-minded perspective, we can actively work toward creating connections to encourage understanding, empathy, and collaboration.

2. Our interaction with and impact on the natural environment is profoundly influenced by the lens through which we perceive the nonhuman world—comprised of water, animals, and plants. Adopting a narrow-blinded stance to this interaction shapes our behaviors in ways that have significant cost implications for environmental well-being. Humans' disdain for the natural environment manifests in seemingly inconsequential actions such as consumption choices, disposal activities, and how

we engage with and perceive animals and our waterways. An approach that encourages us to examine these decisions more carefully might reveal the profound impact of our cognitive processes on the environment and the intricacies of how our thinking influences choices related to purchasing or abstaining and consuming or avoiding.

3. Business activities shaped by narrow-blinded thinking have a significant impact on many communities. Many commercial entities hold a singular view that stems from a profit motive. In such instances, commercial gain has been the priority, and all other considerations are viewed with contempt, sometimes at the expense of the environment and the community. Even though there is a growing emphasis on holistic corporate evaluations and a broader understanding of the impact of business operations on society, there's greater need still to develop an improved symbiotic relationship between businesses and communities. As stakeholders increasingly demand accountability and transparency, a renewed way of thinking about venturing activities could aid in the trajectory of business operations; one that is regarded as responsible and integrated, and embodies the evolving roles and landscape of businesses within the social fabric of society.

4. The impact of narrow-blinded thinking comes into clear focus when examining how some leaders guide and oversee their communities. Such influence permeates various aspects of governance, ranging from the formulation of policies to critical decisions regarding trade, bank rates, and strategic investments. The costs incurred due to a one-sided perspective can manifest in policies lacking foresight, financial decisions prioritizing short-term gains over long-term stability, and strategic investments neglecting the broader implications for the community and the environment. Offering an approach for leaders to critically assess their decisions may provide an

off-ramp from these sorts of policies and actions that fail to address the complexities of contemporary challenges. It could also help leaders make better trade decisions, where a narrow focus on immediate gains may result in missed opportunities for fostering equitable international relationships and promoting global stability.

The Crazy Professor

The irony of a university professor embarking on a journey to address the cost of narrow-blindedness is not lost on me. Surrounded by scores of studies illustrating the impact of narrow teaching practices on student outcomes, I'm well aware that we professors might have a penchant for peddling nonsense and sprinkling a dash of contempt into the mix. The title of this chapter echoes through the hallowed halls where academics essentially declare from their ivory towers, "I am right, and they are wrong." It's shocking, indeed. Despite their four-to-six-year PhD pilgrimage into a specific niche, some professors seem to believe they hold the keys to the universe—a PhD about everything, anyone?

To set the record straight, this book is no run-of-the-mill professorial pontification. Instead, it is a collection of lighthearted stories and a sprinkle of research findings, all orbiting the nucleus of the book's core idea: We need strategies for tackling the most pressing problem of our generation, the narrow-blinded thinking that only leads to the abyss of contempt. The good news is that I have found another route. And here's the kicker—I've road-tested these tips myself, in my consulting gigs and with my students. Let me tell you, success followed.

Narrow-blindedness and its more serious form, contempt, love to play peek-a-boo in the realms of education, business, politics, and international work. And let's quash the notion that this is merely an American pastime—it is a global issue. Having traversed through Ireland, Canada, the US, and forty other countries for education and work, I've seen the unmistakable footprints of narrow-blindedness and contempt in Asia, Australasia, Europe, South-Central America—you name it.

But you might wonder, is the outcome of narrow-blinded thinking, which fuels contempt, truly such a colossal problem? According to Arthur Brooks, the virtuoso Harvard social scientist, musician, and columnist, it's grim. In his *New York Times* article from March 2019, he suggested America's biggest woe isn't inclusivity or intolerance but—you guessed it—contempt, and our inability to see alternative perspectives.[3] I prefer to see narrow-blindedness and contempt as a tax—an unnecessary burden on our collective intellect and not one that funds particularly good results. Yet, fear not, for this book is your semi-comedic guide to a tax deferral strategy. Follow along to learn how to navigate the maze, dodge the pitfalls, and find the levity in our journey to a world where narrow-blinded thinking and contempt are relics of the past.

Context Before We Set Out

Generally speaking, I don't believe that people inherently resist the idea of embracing an alternative perspective. Instead, I believe this perceived resistance often stems from a lack of understanding about how to process and make sense of the unfamiliar. It's a matter of having the right tools to avoid narrow-blindedness, or not knowing how to respond in a way other than rejection.

Unfortunately, this lack of comprehension sets off a chain reaction. It begins innocuously enough with mere disagreement, visible facial contortions, and disengagement, but swiftly descends into the flurry of finger pointing and ad hominem attacks. The escalation of hostilities continues unabated until an impasse is reached and someone exits the conversation with a few rude parting words—whispers under the breath about the other person being a total varmint. Does this sort of mudslinging event sound familiar? If it does, rest assured, you're not alone in experiencing this all-too-predictable interaction. The toll it takes, both emotionally and socially, can be quite significant.

Narrow-blinded thinking is not merely a failure to grasp the logic of something different; it is neglecting to judiciously process alternative perspectives. The aftermath of such thinking breeds an unwavering conviction that the perceived "other" is the root of the problem. This mindset has become an escalating pandemic, evident in the growing difficulty of engaging in political discussions, in both familial and social spheres, without seemingly inevitable conflict.

Unfortunately, it feels like the days of civil discourse, healthy debates, and constructive discussions are gone. Instead, expressing a viewpoint divergent from the collective consensus feels akin to inciting a protest or spurring a riot. Metaphorically, if not literally, individuals in conflict engage in acts of looting, vandalism, and, in extreme cases, causing harm to others. All these actions serve as a loud proclamation: "I am right, and you are wrong. And we don't need to work through this together."

Even I must confess to falling into this thinking culvert, albeit without the physical manifestations of protests, graffiti, or riots. Witnessing firsthand the detrimental consequences of this divisive approach to thinking, and grappling with the associated costs, prompted me to embark on the writing of this book.

To be clear, my intended audience for this book is not confined solely to traditional students; rather, it is aimed at a diverse array of individuals eager to learn. This includes current or aspiring leaders, educators, business owners, politicians, and even the uncle who is at risk of being disinvited from Thanksgiving dinner. The mission is clear: to dismantle the barriers erected by narrow-blinded thinking by mapping an alternative route of open-minded, constructive, and logical thinking.

A Road Map for the Reader

Narrow-blindedness and its close companion, contempt, are serious issues. Despite the gravity of the subject, I've opted for a somewhat lighthearted and humorous approach. Why? Perhaps it's rooted in my satirical personality, as I view much of life through the lens of comedy—a hat on a hat. I've always found enjoyment in a good comedic piece, recognizing that great comedy often carries a thread of truth. Moreover, I believe comedy serves as a bridge between differing opinions and conflicts, whether it's found in a comic strip or a joke delivered by a stand-up comedian. Even when I'm the target of a joke, I appreciate the inherent truth at the core of comedic expression.

Following Einstein's cue on the importance of simplicity, I present a simple drawing outlining the flow of this book on overcoming narrow-blinded thinking for the purpose of positive impact. As you navigate through the book, keep in mind the overarching framework or route is the 3T model: think, talk about it, and take action. You're free to explore the chapters in any order you prefer, as each section will clarify a specific facet of the 3T model.

Figure 0.1

Think
Talk about it
Take action

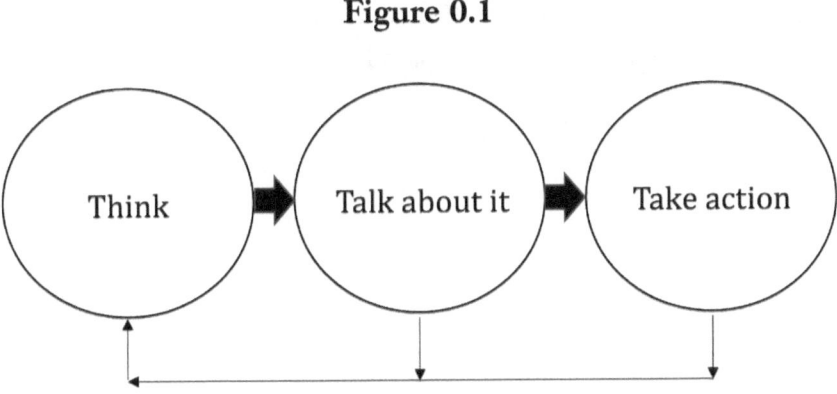

The 3T model to combat narrow-blindedness and contempt.

While the concept of the 3T may seem straightforward, its implementation can prove remarkably challenging. However, with a bit of guidance, rest assured even you can apply these techniques effectively. The key is to balance and link the three. Often, there's an abundance of talk without corresponding action—a domain where the hypocritical armchair coach thrives. On the other hand, some are eager to expound their views without first engaging in careful analysis or thoughtful consideration. I am arguing for equal parts of all three.

I firmly believe in George Washington Carver's assertion that "Education is the key that unlocks the golden door to freedom." My goal is to provide individuals, including students, politicians, and business leaders, with a framework to reshape their thinking, enabling them to identify, assess, and capitalize on new opportunities. I harbor this goal because I want to see a reduction in this escalating trend of looking down upon and disparaging those with differing views. Narrow-blinded thinking and contempt contributes to increased polarization, rendering compromise as elusive as finding a unicorn in our backyard. While the prospect of discovering a unicorn in my backyard would be welcomed, I'm not holding my breath.

Whether you choose to utilize one, two, or all the tools presented in these chapters is entirely at your discretion. Some may resonate more with you or prove more effective than others.

I now present a new route or path for you. Enjoy.

THINK!

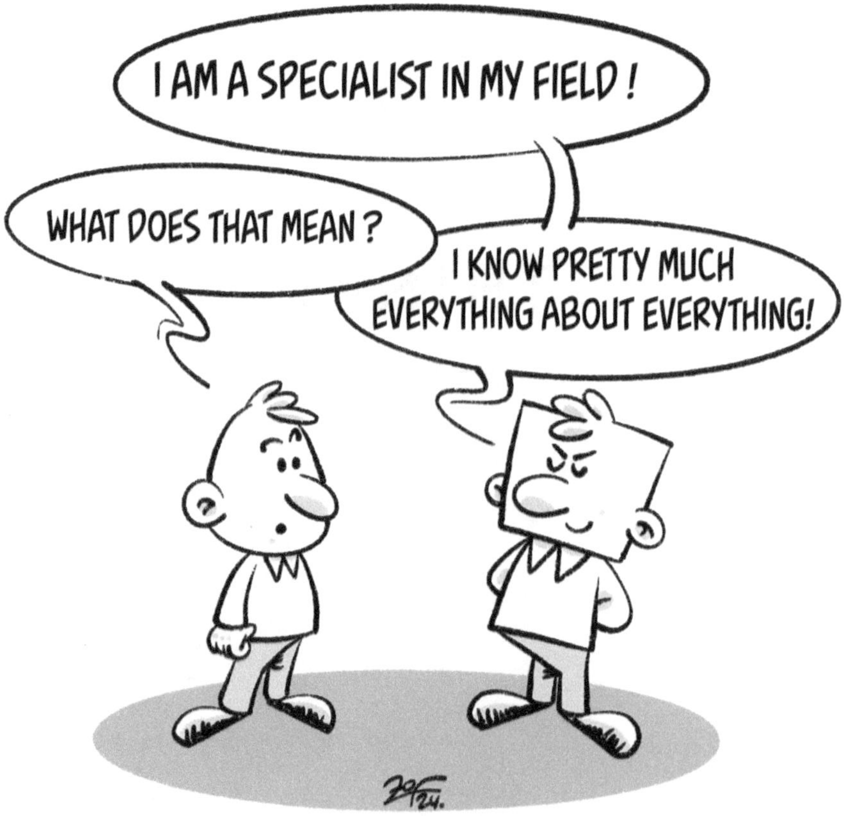
I AM A SPECIALIST IN MY FIELD !
WHAT DOES THAT MEAN ?
I KNOW PRETTY MUCH EVERYTHING ABOUT EVERYTHING!

Chapter One

The Illusion of Knowledge

"You must let go of the illusion . . ."
—The Turtle (from *Kung Fu Panda*)

When Things Don't Go as Expected

When I think of a work-related surprise, I find myself instantly drawn back to a consulting project from earlier in my career. I had been brought in as an external consultant to advise a board of directors that was responsible for steering one of Canada's bigger nonprofit organizations. In some parts of the world, a "nonprofit" is presumed to be a small charity organization, but I can assure you this was a seriously big business enterprise. For a bit of perspective, estimates have charities and nonprofits in Canada contributing around $200 billion to the economic activity of the country. The industry accounts for approximately 8 to 10 percent of the country's gross domestic product and employs some 2.5 million people.[1]

On the first day of my consulting project, I was greeted with a warm reception full of smiles, handshakes, great stories, and excitement. The boardroom was filled with successful business executives who wanted to effect social and economic change. I started off by thanking the group for having me and outlining the brief but focused purpose for the next few days. The ultimate goal was to develop a pseudo-balanced scorecard for the board of directors to link, measure, and report various key performance variables. At the center of the scorecard—from which everything would stem—was the core ethos of the organization, often referred to in business vernacular as the mission and vision of the nonprofit. I thought it was a relatively innocuous start.

So, I passed out some sticky notes and asked each board member to take a few minutes to write down what they perceived to be the mission and vision of the nonprofit. I think a strategy professional (which I am not) would call the mission the "who we are as an organization" statement and the vision the "where we want to be in the future as an organization" statement.

To my surprise, out of the twelve board members, no two produced even tangentially related statements. These were the helmsmen of the organization, responsible for charting the course, yet their perceptions of the organizational identity and direction were totally different from one another's. Needless to say, when their interpretations of the mission and vision were posted on the boardroom's walls for all to see, I only saw shock and horror in their eyes. Which, as you may guess, translated into shock and horror for me. In an instant, these executives realized what they individually thought to be an absolute (the mission and vision) was filled with false assumptions—an illusion, if you will.

As an externally hired consultant, I did what every self-respecting consultant would do and called for a ten-minute break to reflect and pivot from this interesting finding. In those ten minutes, I quickly changed the entire consulting engagement to start at the base of the performance tree, which is to say we spent the remainder of the morning examining each executive's expectations and goals of the nonprofit, so we could focus in on and build a collective understanding of the mission and vision. This had to be done prior to examining their performance measurement system. Just imagine what would have happened if all of these strong-minded individuals had gone ahead with developing a performance measurement for organizational impact without first addressing the obvious perception misalignments.

What I learned from these highly intelligent, passionate, and successful businesspeople was that anyone can be wedded to and simultaneously deceived by their beliefs and perceptions. And much worse, there are the occasions where these illusions of knowledge form the hull of the ship we are steering. As most sailing enthusiasts know, a weak hull can take on water, ending in a sunk ship. This is why having systematic mechanisms to dispel such illusions and misapprehensions is one way to avoid sinking and/or hitting the iceberg of narrow-blinded thinking and contempt.

The Beauty of Magic

Have you ever watched David Blaine perform? David is an illusionist who has been in the magic industry for nearly three decades (perhaps even longer, because I have no idea what he did in his formative years). As a professional magician and a street performer, he has been buried alive, frozen, drowned, and shocked. Breaking Guinness World Records seems like a walk in the park for him. I personally enjoyed it when he ate a wine glass at a party with Arnold Schwarzenegger and regurgitated frogs into a wine glass at a party with Drake. I suppose you could say that I am drawn to wine and magic.

Despite my admiration for David as a craftsman, I am constantly wondering how he does what he does because it is, after all, an illusion. The point is this: I am not inclined to accept magic as something supernatural because there must indeed be something behind the curtain, just like in *The Wizard of Oz*. I just have to *think* about it for a while! It's very much the same with narrow-blinded thinking . . . it requires time to think. So, what do I mean when I say, "Think about it"? How do we do that? One way is to unpack illusions of knowledge by understanding overconfidence and how it works.

Figure 1.1

Talk
about it
1. The illusion
of knowledge
Think
Take action

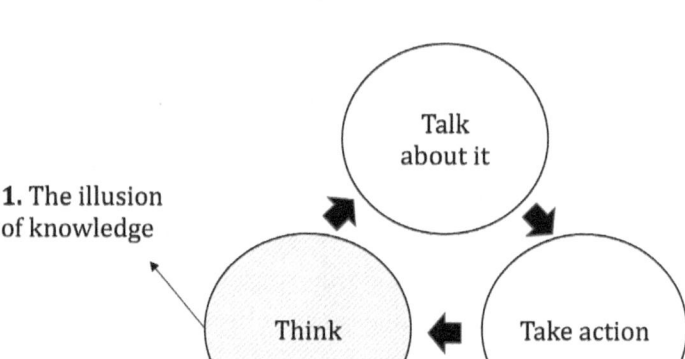

Combating narrow-blinded thinking by overcoming the illusions of knowledge.

We Overestimate What We Know

What do I mean by illusion of knowledge? Well, from time to time, what we think we know is greater than what we actually know. We believe that what we personally perceive is neither an illusion nor magic, and indeed we have discovered the singular truth. (Yes, I am being sarcastic right now.) In this way, we are essentially overestimating what we know. Perhaps a friend of yours says they don't need a map because their sense of direction is really good. Yet, they still get lost, and despite being lost, they wouldn't be caught dead asking for directions. (Is this really a male-related phenomena?) They may even know they are going in the wrong direction but continue along the road, because they cannot bring themselves to admit they are wrong. This is called overcommitment. Or perhaps you know a colleague who is convinced they are smarter than everyone else, despite the absence of any facts to support their genius. Or maybe you have a religious neighbor who claims with absolute conviction and confidence that their theological beliefs are the one and only truth. In these instances, you might even get a side of authoritarian contempt for alternative views.

Many researchers have studied overestimates and overconfidence in different settings, and found relatively similar results. Nobel prizes have been awarded for this domain of research. The evidence from these studies demonstrates we all do this to some extent or another (some more than others). Overconfidence is a real phenomenon, and it is a person's *subjective confidence* in the conclusions they draw (also called judgments). It comes to life in different day-to-day scenarios, such as overestimation of personal performance, overplacement of ourselves relative to others, or overestimation of the accuracy of our opinions and knowledge. As illustrated in the comic at the beginning of this chapter, individuals frequently think they are more correct and more knowledgeable than they actually are. Is there something to the old adage that says, "93 percent of drivers are certain they are above-average drivers"? It seems so, and it likely finds its foundation in overconfidence. The fallacy of our overestimation is comically articulated in the movie *Anchorman* when Brian Fantana says to Ron Burgundy, "They've done studies, you know. Sixty percent of the time, it works every time." But thankfully Ron doesn't succumb to Brian Fantana's overconfidence and responds, "Brian, I'm gonna be honest with you, that smells like pure gasoline." *The Legend of Ron Burgundy* continues.

Try to think of all the times you have witnessed others (or yourself) poorly assess and misalign *subjective* probabilities, whether it was in an estimation, precision, and/or overplacement. It happens when people think they have control when they really don't, or when people underestimate how long it will take to do something. Perhaps it is because we believe a low-probability event will happen simply because it is desirable—"I'll definitely get that job! Who cares that two thousand other people have applied?" Or in the case of our driver example, they are certain they are above average or hold an overly positive belief about themselves. Don't get me wrong, I am generally an optimist, but I must frequently let go of how precise I think my knowledge is on a range of topics.

A Response to Overestimation

It may initially come across as a little depressing that overestimation and overconfidence run rampant and lead to poor judgment and decision-making. Overestimation and overconfidence contribute to narrow-blinded thinking and contempt too. Perhaps we should accept this illusion, bury our heads in the sand, and carry on with the status quo? No way. There are simple and subtle ways to challenge and counteract our tendency toward overestimation and overconfidence.

Early in my career, I was granted a golden opportunity to immerse myself in the realm of economics at an institute in Germany. Despite the pervasive notion that economics is the "dismal science" (a term coined by historian Thomas Carlyle based on Malthus's grim predictions), I've always seen it as a guiding light. This experience, set against the backdrop of Germany's rich cultural history and punctuated by the joyous exploration of its culinary offerings, was transformative for a directionless young academic.

During my time at the institute, the invaluable lesson of "define and defend" became ingrained in my approach to discussions, presentations, and debates. This simple yet powerful concept demands that, at the outset, participants articulate precisely what they are talking about before delving into their supporting evidence. Despite its apparent straightforwardness, close scrutiny of conversations often reveals what I term "logic fractures"—misalignments or uncertainties about the fundamental aspects of what individuals are trying to convey. Just the other day, my friends Rick and Kate asked me to define what I meant by the word "altruism" during a conversation we were having.

Consider a quick experiment. In your next conversation, inquire, "What do you mean by that word or topic?" or "Can you provide more insight into this specific topic, as I'm not entirely clear about it?" or "How does that process happen?" Intentionally asking for definitions signals a genuine interest in learning and engaging with someone's perspective.

Define and Defend: The Big Version

Over the years, the impact of the "define and defend" principle on my graduate students' growth has been nothing short of remarkable. How did this unfold? Through one-on-one academic debates—a distinctive twist on traditional discussions. These debates, while slightly more structured with time constraints and a specific format, share a fundamental premise with traditional group discussions. Importantly, the structured nature of one-on-one debates has the added advantage of tempering the overpowering influence of the loudest voices in the room—those who believe confident rambling is the key to winning.

In the case of my graduate students, the purpose of these academic debates is twofold: to provide them with a platform to practice and build confidence in presenting and arguing in front of an audience—an essential life skill—and to share with their peers the knowledge and perspectives they've acquired while researching contentious topics. The core of these debates revolves around the "define and defend" ethos.

Here's how it works: Students receive a predetermined topic in advance and are assigned opposing sides. For example, one student might be assigned to argue that social and environmental reporting should be mandatory for all publicly accountable enterprises (Side A), while another is set to argue against it (Side B). Each student then prepares their arguments within the defined parameters of the debate.

The showdown unfolds with a head-to-head debate in front of the class. There are distinct stages: opening arguments, where students present their case based on research; cross-examination, an opportunity to question the opposing side and expose weaknesses in their argument; rebuttals, to clarify points or highlight flaws raised during the cross-examination; and closing statements, a response to the debate's trajectory and an overall summary of their position. It is a giant define and defend fest!

One might think academic debates could be stress-inducing, especially for newcomers. Initially, perhaps it is. However, as my students engaged in more debates, they not only became remarkably composed and thoughtful but also transformed the debates into dynamic discussions of differing viewpoints. Most notably, they grew more confident and articulate in their views, all while embracing alternative perspectives and, surprisingly, having a lot of fun.

While not every conversation needs to adopt the rigor of these debates, applying similar principles to everyday discussions can be enlightening. Imagine asking questions like: Can you define that particular topic for me? What evidence led you to your position? Where did you get your supporting evidence? Would you mind if I asked a few questions to understand and perhaps challenge your perspective further? Could I share my perspective and evidence with you?

Define and Defend: Alternative Perspectives

Here is another example of the define and defend idea. Consider the 1978 Ford Pinto recall, where approximately 1.5 million cars out of 12.5 million were recalled due to a design flaw making them susceptible to fire in collisions.[2] Evidence indicated Ford's awareness of the issue, leading many to condemn such duplicitous behavior as unconscionable, seemingly beyond debate.

Enter Michael Sandel, a Harvard Law School professor who turns this grotesque Ford situation into a platform for thoughtful debate and dialogue, employing Jeremy Bentham's logic. Bentham suggests the measure of right and wrong should prioritize the greatest happiness for the greatest number of people. Sandel challenges his students to explore and define what maximizing happiness truly means, delving into the merits and shortcomings of cost-benefit calculations, a nuanced understanding of happiness over suffering, and the potentially incommensurable aspects of human life. This approach aims to foster thought-provoking dialogue enriched with socially desirable and undesirable contentions, encouraging active listening and reflection on diverse perspectives.

The essence of this example serves three purposes. First, it underscores that respectful debate is not synonymous with contempt, emphasizing the importance of maintaining civility in discussions (just like the two old Irish guys at the pub). Second, it highlights the potential consequences if narrow-blindedness and contempt were granted entry at the onset of the debate—insights would be lost, and the conversation could spiral downward. Third, while not excusing Ford's actions, it demonstrates the power of dialogue and debate, when grounded in a particular definition (e.g., Jeremy Bentham's measure of right and wrong), to offer a potent strategy for new perspectives.

Try it. In your next "spicy" conversation with someone who is exhibiting contempt, ask: (1) "Could you elaborate on your perspective? Can you define what you're talking about?" (Feel free to seek more clarity through examples.) (2) "Where did you find the supporting evidence for your viewpoint?"

Approach it with genuine care and sincerity, not to prove them wrong. Take a page from Theodore Roosevelt: "Nobody cares how much you know until they know how much you care."

Dialing It Down a Few Notches

In 2013 Philip Fernbach and his colleagues at the University of Colorado conducted a fascinating study.[3] They were interested in reducing extreme political attitudes about particularly complex policies. The crux of Fernbach and his colleagues' research paper was a gallant one. Their starting point was the view that we generally don't know as much as we think we do, but they were particularly interested in the question of how we get people to see the flaws in their logic and dial down their strong viewpoints on such matters.

So, Fernbach and his colleagues ran a few different and really cool experiments to see if individuals were near delusional about their level of knowledge around a topic they hold dear. What they found was something rather interesting. Over the course of three separate experiments, they asked people to explain the detailed mechanics behind the policy they felt so strongly about (e.g., how it worked and what the process was). By asking for a written mechanistic explanation, they found the individuals in the experiments significantly reduced their overall compunction that they knew everything about a policy and moved toward more moderate views. As the old *Saturday Night Live* skit goes, it got them to "simmer down now." Fernbach and his colleagues called this illusion of knowledge "explanatory depth," as it took being asked to explain something for these individuals to realize their own limited understanding.

These researchers also found that simply asking people in the experiment to give their reasons (instead of the mechanistic logic) for their views on the policy resulted in no significant change in their attitude toward the topic. Said another way, asking for reasons why someone supports or believes in something is way less powerful than asking people to explain how something works or what the processes are.

I can think of two ways to interpret these findings. The first is that people's illusions of knowledge about the processes underlying certain policies become a barrier to seeing alternatives and likely an impediment to compromise. The second is that asking people to explain what they understand, namely the mechanism or process behind their view (e.g., A causes B, B causes C, and C causes D), opens the door to alternatives because after realizing their knowledge is not as complete as they thought, they may be willing to step out of their entrenched views. Perhaps this is a mechanism that encourages people to dial it down a few notches, thereby reducing narrow-blinded thinking and in turn contempt.

Imagine what might happen if you ask and give time, listen carefully, and repeat back what people say as they explain how they think something works. I have seen a wonderful tempering of beliefs

Chapter One: The Illusion of Knowledge

when this is done. Recently my wife asked me to explain the mechanisms behind the statistical results of a study from the perspective of the results table. She asked, "What is this saying? What does this mean? How does this work?" I tried to explain, only to realize I took many of the statistical mechanisms for granted. We went back and looked at them together. Who would have thought statistics could be so much fun!

Mechanistic logic can also be called A-B-C-D logic. The premise is that A causes B, which causes C, which causes D. How about an example in practice? In a large research study conducted within the US, two friends and I were examining the impacts of tax policy on the purchase of electric vehicles. We set up an experiment whereby people were asked about a vehicle purchase. Including sales tax, the estimated total price of the new gas-powered car would be $25,000 and the total price of the new electric-powered car would be $34,000. We checked to ensure these costs were possible with a non-luxury electric car.

Some of our test subjects were assessed a tax penalty of $3,000 (a new state tax surcharge on gas-powered cars to encourage individuals to reduce carbon dioxide emissions) and others were given a tax incentive of $3,000 (a new state tax incentive on electric-powered cars to encourage individuals to reduce carbon dioxide emissions).

We were particularly interested in whether or not providing an A-B-C-D logic explanation, when paired with the tax penalty or tax incentive, would motivate purchase decisions. Here is an example of a mechanistic argument from our study:

> Scientific studies have established that since 1900, the air temperature on Earth has risen almost 2 degrees. A large part of the temperature increase on Earth is caused by humans burning fossil fuels. Burning fossil fuels produces carbon dioxide, a heat trapping gas, that when released into the atmosphere increases Earth's air temperature. One of the biggest causes of

carbon dioxide is gas-powered vehicles. Carbon dioxide from gas-powered vehicle emissions increases the Earth's air temperature, which leads to global changes in precipitation, snow and ice melt, and extreme weather, such as heavy rains, heat waves, and severe storms. But the good news is that we can change these environmental impacts with our purchase decisions. Increasing the number of electric vehicles will slow the warming of the Earth, caused largely by carbon dioxide being released from gas-powered vehicles. Therefore, I support the $3,000 sales tax incentive that individuals will receive on the purchase of electric-powered vehicles because it will decrease the cost of electric cars and encourage more individuals to purchase electric-powered vehicles.[4]

The point here was whether or not study participants agreed with the logic presented in this statement. I also understand behavioral research has shortcomings too. Recent empirical evidence—in combination with other similar studies examining this topic—suggest there might be something to the benefits of utilizing mechanistic logic. In our study, providing individuals with A-B-C-D logic did seem to impact people's behavior, when compared to the control group that received no such prompts. Perhaps this provides some evidence that explanations may help to minimize overconfidence and overcommitment to a particular position.

Sinek and *Hot Ones*

Okay, so how do you avoid the awkwardness that ensues if you ask someone to write out their logic? As much as I would like to do the paper and pencil test, I can't imagine being in the middle of a heated family debate on politics, slapping down a pencil and notebook, and asking my family members to write out their causal understandings of foreign policy. Hilarious, but weird. There is another way to elucidate causal mechanism knowledge: ask first-rate questions about the how and why of things.

Asking revealing questions (of the how and why sort) probes logic in subtle ways and may be another avenue toward achieving the outcomes described by Fernbach and colleagues. I admire Simon Sinek's ability to ask amazing questions from a corporate strategy standpoint. In his book *Start with Why*, he asks a simple but necessary question: "Why do only a few companies and leaders really change the world while the others exist?" The answer, he says, is that they inspire action by asking a critically important evaluative question to find the *why* behind all their efforts. What is the logic or mechanism of their efforts? Sinek's ability to distill the *why* question has implications for how we communicate the relationships between things to our teams, customers, and external world. He terms this the *why* of enduring enterprises.

Sinek takes another formidable angle on probing questions about the rules of the game (how things work, a.k.a. the mechanism). He explains this in terms of finite games and infinite games. Finite games being defined by getting to the end of the game and winning with static rules, as opposed to infinite games, where the goal is to keep going rather than winning, to expand horizons and inspire conversation and resiliency. In a lot of ways, Sinek focuses on the mindset of questioning how something works.

Another entrepreneur who changes the dynamic of interactions through great questions is Sean Evans. Sean is the creator and host of the TV series *Hot Ones*. This show is hilarious because Sean invites big-name celebrities onto his set to eat progressively hotter chicken wings that are off the chart insane, all while interviewing these persons of interest. I like making hot sauce, so I am naturally drawn to the premise of this show. If you listen closely, he also garners amazing insights because of his outstanding questions. I'll never forget the episode where Dr. Ken Jeong came on the show. It is a must-watch. Dr. Ken actually complimented Sean for the quality and thoughtfulness of his questions because it provided him with an on-ramp to explain how something worked and to highlight the big inflection points in the trajectory of his career. I still laugh when I see the blend of hot-wing-eating pain, superb questions, and Dr. Ken saying, "Fuck you, Sean, you warm me up [with great questions], I really thought we were about to be friends, and now I am back in the gutter of my hatred for Sean Evans." Not only have I been in tears laughing from this show, I have learned a lot about the quality of questions from Sean. His poise under the extreme duress of crazy hot chicken wings while asking thoughtful questions to get a deeper understanding of his guests is true artistry. His line of questioning, under any conditions but especially these, takes practice and is also a good yet unconventional model for others to follow. I wonder what would happen if Sinek and Evans worked together on a hot wings for business leaders podcast . . .

Causal Loops

There is an alternative approach to shed light on the idea of A-B-C-D logic in a business setting. A-B-C-D logic (or mechanistic logic) is sometimes referred to as causal logic—it traces how one thing impacts another thing, which impacts another thing. I remember working on a causal project with a large nonprofit healthcare provider out West. The findings ended up getting published in an academic journal because they were novel in this particular setting. Interestingly the genesis of the project was more about asking questions (hopefully like Sean's) to get at senior management's logic of how their business worked. My co-researchers and I were working with a community health business, a rather large operation, incorporating medical, dental, mental health, and a litany of other health-related services. The organization was stacked with an impressive group of people and led by a savvy and thoughtful CEO. However, many members of the management team held different beliefs about how their organization functioned (how it worked) to achieve its ultimate goals. I also don't believe they shared the same set of organizational goals, which is not uncommon in big businesses.

Our research team used a method called causal modeling, which is a fancy way of saying we got the entire executive team in a room (over multiple sessions) to map out and agree on the logic of how their critical performance variables dynamically and recursively affected each other. It was, as Fernbach and colleagues would say, the development of a mechanistic explanation (A causes B, B causes C, C causes D)—or, as I say, how one thing impacts another thing, which impacts another thing.

We did this to offer the team at the healthcare facility a path to identify key points of leverage for organizational action. It was very successful because, to the surprise of the executives, it challenged their logic, clarified causal relationships, and identified new pathways for organizational action. What was cool about the process was it revealed assumptions, choices, and complexities and so helped the healthcare organization recognize possible strategic opportunities. Here are a few comments from the executives who participated in the study:

> "The representation also showed causal relations depicting that serving more patients with adequate insurance could increase revenue, decreasing CHP's dependence on grants, and possibly leading to increased compensation for healthcare providers (the lower left of the causal diagram)."

> "This [our current business model] is not a sustainable business model. We try to solve everything but [don't] get paid for it."

> "Our current model is hopeless when we look at the causal loops."

> "We will always have less [revenue available] than we want."

"Increasing pay [for example] may put pressure on these other things."

The end causal map is presented in Figure 1.2.[5] The executives made some important changes to their logic and business model because they better understood how things worked (the mechanistic logic). What was uniquely interesting to me was how the process of drawing out the relationships converted the implicit assumptions and estimations into clear, explicit events. After we collectively agreed on the causal model, I heard great dialogue about assumptions, estimations, and renewed perspectives. I am not saying one has to get into this level of granular causal details in all discussions of all topics, but the options are limitless and very helpful if the goal is to counteract narrow-blindedness.

Figure 1.2

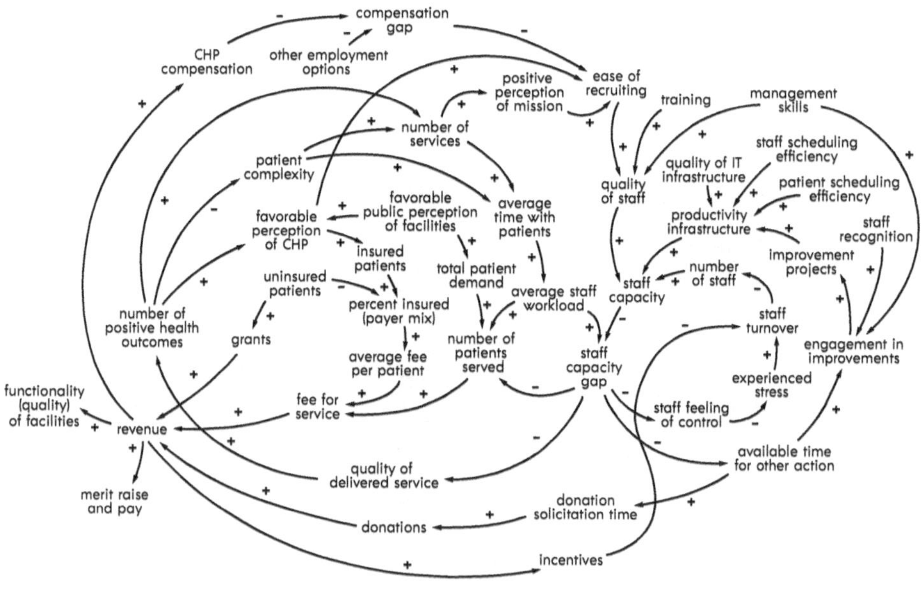

Causal logic at work.

Asking Questions about How Something Works

How can you engage in debate in a non-polarizing way? Take a news reporter approach. In my mind, a key attribute that differentiates award-winning news reporters from mediocre or terrible news reporters is how they go about their reporting assignment—their questions, their energy for inquisition, and the depths they go to in an effort to understand how something works. Journalist and author Malcolm Gladwell is a genius at this approach. His research savvy is next level! He is uber inquisitive, he digs until he understands how things work, and he seeks knowledge on the ground level from people who live the experience. During his entire research journey, he continues to refine his questions. He is a total master at the process.

I tried this approach when I became interested in the tax exemptions given to nonprofits. Motivated by a news story about the abuse of tax-exempt status by registered nonprofits, a close friend and I asked a simple question: When do tax-exempt nonprofits detract value from society? We surveyed fifteen years of tax-exempt nonprofit scholarships spanning across nine disciplines. It was a collection of mechanistic logics (A causes B) from multiple perspectives. As a result, we found and showed a long history of collective mechanistic arguments, which we funneled into three buckets: policy-making and regulation intemperance, nonprofit management and governance distraction, and detection and prosecution inconsistencies. Our logic and evidence explained when and why tax-exempt nonprofits can detract value from society. Can this logic be challenged? Absolutely. But the mechanistic logic is written for others to read and discuss, rather than as a mere pontification of views.[6]

Imagine you were given a chance to report on something that was really exciting and interesting to you. What topic or questions would you research and write about? What experts would you interview? What questions would you ask? What do you think you currently know on the topic, and what is unclear to you? How and why did this event (or events) happen? How would you go about formulating the story arc of this major event? My guess is a reporter like Gladwell would start by asking a simple and interesting question to which he does not know the answer, then he would ask the experts and interviewees to define and defend what they believe.

Combating narrow-blinded thinking by overcoming the illusions of knowledge is the point of this chapter. The Mexican poet, essayist, novelist, and short story writer José Emilio Pacheco said it well when he once commented, "We are all hypocrites. We cannot see ourselves or judge ourselves the way we see and judge others." Unfortunately, this type of hypocrisy sneaks into assessments of our knowledge and closes the door to new perspectives and opportunities. The good news is we can combat the illusion of knowledge that leads to narrow-blinded thinking. Asking questions with clinical precision and genuinely listening as others explain their mechanistic logic is a measured beginning that can pull back the big red curtain of the illusion.

 **Defining and explaining helps to explore the depth of understanding. Great questions are the guide en route.**

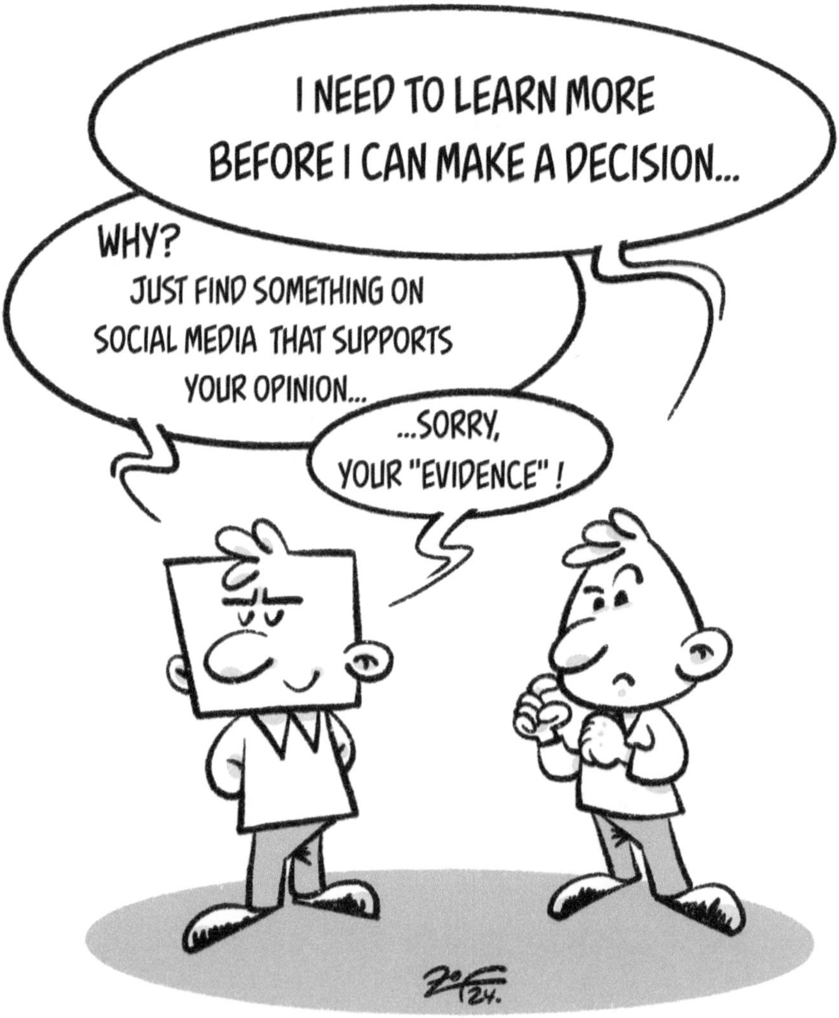
I NEED TO LEARN MORE BEFORE I CAN MAKE A DECISION...
WHY? JUST FIND SOMETHING ON SOCIAL MEDIA THAT SUPPORTS YOUR OPINION...
...SORRY, YOUR "EVIDENCE"!

Chapter Two

"Fake News" . . . and My Truth

> "The fact that an opinion has been widely held is no evidence whatever that it is not utterly absurd."
> —Bertrand Russell

Hot Off the Press

"Fake news" is a relatively new phrase. Yet the idea behind it has been around for quite some time. In the 1700s, news printers fabricated a story that King George II was ill as a destabilizing tactic. In the 1800s, the London stock market shot upward when contrived reports of peace with France were presented to the public. In August of 1835, the *New York Sun* published a series of articles about the supposed discovery of life on the moon. In June of 1897, Mark Twain chuckled about misinformation in the news that he was dying in poverty. As World War I destroyed Europe, more than one news outlet published accounts from sources who claimed to have visited cadaver processing plants in Germany, where glycerin was extracted from the corpses of the fallen to make soap and margarine.

These are but a few examples of deceptive media news reports, and they do not do justice to the extent of the problem of fake news. Whether intentional or unintentional, distortions of events happen on the daily. My guess is that you're not surprised to hear this. I am definitely not. Perhaps you have come to accept (but dislike) deceptive practices in the news, in politics, and in corporate advertising. Well, I can't blame you. It's annoying having to sift through the garbage. Recently, somebody told me they'd read that eating Oreos makes you thin and I got the impression they truly believed their source!

So, what can we do? Well, I am not convinced we should reorient our thinking to expect that everything is a lie. Doing so would be a bit too extreme, but exercising some healthy skepticism might be a good start. How do we do that? Many of our daily interactions and dialogues are based on a subset of knowledge boundaries. I call this the garage decision-making problem. Imagine a clean and organized garage. Sports equipment, storage boxes, and tools are all in the right place, frequently used, cleaned, and organized. Now imagine the alternative, a cluttered mess of a garage. Half-open garbage bags are strewn everywhere. Old, broken, and unused junk is all over the place. Soggy, torn, and unlabeled storage boxes litter the place like a back alley. How could you find anything in this dump? How could anyone organize their thoughts and find what they need in order to articulate their views with a mind this messy? This is the garage decision-making problem.

Boundary conditions are the type of garage we keep and use to inform decision-making. It is the storage of our evidence. Some of these boundaries are exceedingly sloppy and others are pristine. What tools and equipment you have in your garage, how frequently you use them, and the extent to which you have all items organized are the boundaries of decision-making.

As we think about things, the trick is to be able to understand boundary conditions—the quality and organization of our evidence.

Don't Give That Student a Reference!

I have been working in the US for over a decade. The genesis of this particular decade of my US life was trying to get tenure as a university professor out West (which I did). Then I moved to the New England region to be closer to my family in Eastern Canada. It wasn't until my wife and I drove cross-country with our two schnauzer dogs (aptly named Keebler and Tetley, after the cookie and tea elves) for this move that I truly grasped the sheer size and variety of landscapes within this country. Each region had its own style of food, expressions, accents, and way of living. The rural farming and the big-city living were quite a contrast. To me it was like many little countries within one country. I think Steinbeck was on point, in his book *Travels with Charlie*, when he described the country as diverse and fascinating. As we drove, I wondered if being a professor out West would be different than being a professor in the East. The good news is I had forty-plus hours of driving to reflect on that question.

A common thread, regardless of where I move, is my occupation as a university professor. It has been a rewarding job! Best of all, it is transferable from state to state. In this sense, I don't have to get recertified or pass any board exams to practice in a new state. A PhD transfers unlike certifications in fields like medicine or law, for which you have to pass board exams in each state. The job mobility of a professor is great. As a university faculty member, it's as easy as getting another job offer and moving to another institution.

One of the most gratifying parts of being a faculty member has been helping students prepare for the workforce. The process requires talking with students about opportunities, helping them with their resumes, introducing them to employers for internship opportunities, and connecting them with others for full-time jobs in their chosen profession. Even though I largely focus on accounting, tax, and finance jobs, in my estimation what follows is applicable to a range of university disciplines.

What has amazed me during my time in the US is the heavy focus on student grade point averages as the core barometer for job readiness and placement. It is much the same in many Asian nations where one's scholastic test scores determine much, if not all, of the job placement outcomes. This was vividly brought to my attention when a faculty member came rushing into my office (without knocking or saying hello; yes, a rather brash individual) and launched into a barrage of commentary. "Ed, you cannot give a reference for this big consulting job if a student has less than a 3.7 GPA! Totally unacceptable." (In case you are unaware, GPA stands for grade point average, and is used in the US to determine a number-to-letter grade equivalency. For example, a 3.7 GPA equates to around an A- average on all course work.)

My response to my abrasive colleague was, "Oh, I was not aware that this was the policy. Can you explain why?" In my mind, I was also thinking of asking why she was so hostile and angry, or if she would like to screen all my reference selections in the future, but I didn't. My goal was to understand the state of her garage thinking.

Instead of a cogent set of evidence, this colleague told me, in no uncertain terms, that my recommendation was not good. My colleague's view was that this particular student wasn't the "best of the best." Even though this phrase "best of the best" sounded cool, I still struggled to understand what it really meant, so I asked what it was about this student that signaled something other than the "best of the best." My query was followed with a blank face. They knew nothing about the student (they had never had this student in their class). They only knew their GPA. My view was that solid grades, a leader of a successful varsity team, and a dedication to serving others in the community was worthy of a reference. I also had weekly interactions with this particular student in my class—interactions that informed my opinion of their character. In the case of my colleague, none of this mattered because the student didn't have a 3.7 GPA.

Needless to say, I was a bit befuddled by this interaction and my coworker's assessment. For a moment I wondered if I was wrong, and perhaps grade point average was truly the only necessary predictor for jobs in accounting and tax consulting. It got me thinking. If this was the case, wow, did I ever get lucky in my career! If GPA was the only measure, I think I would have missed out on a lot of job opportunities during my formative years.

I decided to get two other data points on the matter. I turned to a leading scholar in the field of organizational psychology and an audit expert. I figured organizational psychology and auditing were critical knowledge sets when it came to uncovering insights on individuals and their behavior. I asked them, what does the current literature say about personnel selection criteria? Was I off the mark with my assessment of this particular student? Was the GPA barometer of 3.7 correct?

As I explained the encounter with my gruff coworker, my goal was to disprove my own logic. It just so happened that in this instance, I couldn't. One colleague (and expert in selection criteria) recounted the multitude of characteristics that make up selection factors, the least of which is GPA. These factors included job experience, life circumstances, personal character, focus, drive, interests, and so much more. All of these factors weigh into and help determine what constitutes a good and successful employee.

Here is what I learned from my interactions with the abrasive coworker, the psychologist, and the auditor. First, it is not uncommon to have entrenched views, and entrenched views can blind us to objective facts. Second, pleading a lack of awareness on what research has to say on a topic is like telling a police officer you shouldn't get a ticket because you were unaware of the speed limit—not much of a defense. There is a litany of scholars who want to share their findings to inform people's decisions; all you have to do is look and ask. And finally, just because someone yells at you or speaks in an aggressive tone doesn't mean they are right. My grumpy and aggressive coworker was very well known for this approach.

As a side note, the student did get the job!

The point is that narrow-blinded thinking occurs when individuals don't use evidence or seek information that only supports their preexisting perspectives. I must report that this decision-making fallacy is known as a confirmation bias. Simply put, there is a need to fine-tune our approach to examining evidence. Judicious evaluation of evidence is the goal, and sound evidence makes for an organized garage in your mind!

Birds Aren't Real

When I reflect on the 3.7 GPA comment, I am instantly reminded of Bertrand Russell's quote: "An opinion that is widely held is no evidence whatever that it is not utterly absurd." It is precisely where lack of evidence takes root. Take the case of a 2017 college dropout named Peter McIndoe, who started a movement he called "Birds Aren't Real." His main contention was that birds were exterminated in the 1950s and 1960s by the government and replaced with lookalike robots that were intended to gather information on citizens. Apparently, these drone-birds also sit on power lines to recharge.

When "Birds Aren't Real" exploded in popularity and support, McIndoe finally reported the entire thing was a hoax perpetrated in response to a world where the absence of facts and misinformation prevailed. It was his way of fighting the madness of what constitutes evidence with sheer lunacy. "Birds Aren't Real" has created a cultlike following—though most followers don't actually believe birds are drones, but rather see a need to call out baseless claims and protests with no understanding of reality.

Responding to absurd dogmas with comedy does have its upside. It definitely suits my personality, but may not be effective in all settings. In place of comedy, I would offer research-based evidence as a more diplomatic approach (even though it is far less funny than a "Birds Aren't Real" approach). By research-based, I mean seeking out the best available research in the field with the explicit intent to increase confidence in the decision made. How about a few examples of research-based evidence insights? You may have heard of Dr. Jane Goodall, who lived with wild chimpanzees in Tanzania for long stretches in order to understand and offer insights on why both animals and humans behave in certain ways. Or massive empirical studies run by global health organizations to research the social determinants of health over long periods of time. Or Thor Heyerdahl, who in 1947 sailed a hand-built vessel from Peru across the Pacific Ocean to the Tuamotu Islands to demonstrate that ancient people could make long sea voyages. All of these constitute evidence to some extent or another. The reality is that many of us will never live in Tanzania, be a statistician working on health data, or sail across oceans to test a theory. However, we can be the person who finds and uses evidence-based data in a judicious way!

If you haven't read the book *Guns, Germs, and Steel* by Jared Diamond, you should pick up a copy. It is an exemplary demonstration of how multiple aspects of evidence can be used to answer a question with the utmost elegance. The particular question Diamond asks, and then answers, is why some societies developed faster and sustained themselves longer than others, and perhaps to a secondary extent, why some societies conquered others. To answer the question, Diamond went into significant detail, explaining the historical and geographical aspects of migration, agriculture, food production, domestication of animals, environmental qualities, health technology, social structure, immunity to deadly diseases, written language, inventions, power structures, and political centralization. All served the purpose of effectively answering his question and providing impressive evidence.

The world of evidence is vast, and we must venture into it for the purpose of combating narrow-blinded thinking. Now let's unpack an approach to tackle this leg of the journey.

Figure 2.1

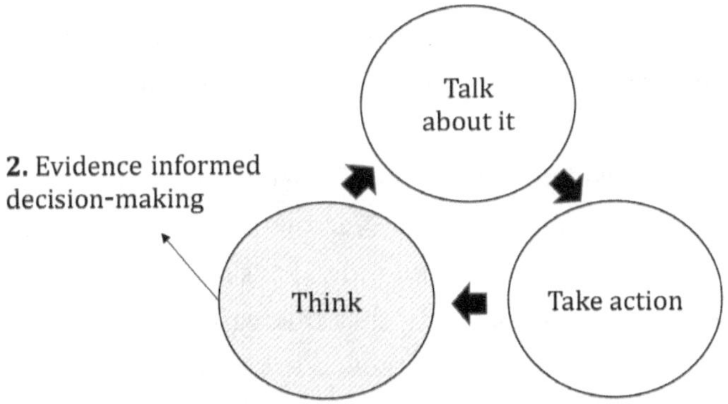

2. Evidence informed decision-making

Talk about it

Think

Take action

Combating narrow-blinded thinking through evidence-informed thinking.

What Constitutes Evidence?

How about a framework for thinking about evidence that might prove helpful? I turn to the concept of evidence-based decision-making by Dr. Denise Rousseau, professor of Organizational Behavior and Public Policy at Carnegie Mellon University. Her work in organizational psychology has contributed to some of the most foundational insights on contract theory, idiosyncratic deals, and perhaps most notably, evidence-based management. For an extended description of evidence-based management, you can visit the Center for Evidence-Based Management, which she co-founded with Eric Barends.[1] I'll give you a brief synopsis.

Despite my general orientation toward business research (because it is my domain of expertise), evidence-based management extends well beyond the boundaries of my discipline. In fact, this type of thinking has existed for many decades in the practice of medicine and law. For example, in medicine, medical professionals use patient histories to understand the specifics of each patient's case and doctors draw on their vast experience with patients who have similar histories and medical issues to inform their decisions. The best doctors examine published research frequently in their area of disease. For treatments, doctors experiment with a range of approaches to solve patient ailments.

In a straightforward and pragmatic way, evidence-based practice is defined as "the science-informed practice of management in which ethics and stakeholder concerns, practitioner judgment and expertise, local data and experimentation, and principles derived through formal research are each considered critically and used to inform decision-making."[2]

A goal of evidence-based decision-making is to close the gap between research and practice. Narrow-blindedness emerges from organizations, governments, and individuals not utilizing the best evidence available. It is not likely that this gap will close entirely, but there are several ways we can reduce it significantly when it comes to poor decision-making and contempt. I will say that judicious decision-making takes time; however, it is very rewarding. One of the main benefits I have found in using this way of thinking is that you begin to critically appraise information and commentary you encounter in everyday interactions.

What does evidence-based thinking look like in practice? Say you want to think more carefully about a particular topic. Here are four approaches that you as a decision-maker can use; these approaches can be employed individually or in unison. First, you can take time to understand the values and concerns of people who may be affected by your decision. Second, you can reach out to professionals to learn from expert experience and judgment. Third, you can gather data, facts, and insights about the specific question. And finally, fourth, you can look to studies on the particular topic that are published in academic journals. With evidence drawn from all four of these inputs, you then think really hard about the decision. Sounds exhausting, right? It is. But it is so much fun to debunk a myth or a misunderstanding through critical appraisal—much more than it is to make a half-baked decision. Essentially, evidence-based thinking insulates against blind acceptance of unsubstantiated commentary—commentary that can deeply shape the way we think about our interactions and the world around us.

Why should we try to focus on the best available evidence? Because it will likely improve our perspectives across the range of issues by reducing narrow-blinded thinking and subsequent contempt. Thus it will also foster support for more productive, important, and well-informed decisions. Let's say you are really interested in marine biology and want to understand the latest research on water quality and water systems. Or perhaps you want to better understand the staggering impact humans have on water quality around the world. Dr. Andrea Rinaldo's research would pop up quickly, putting a plethora of evidence right at your fingertips. From this evidence, you could learn about protecting biodiversity and stemming the spread of disease in an effort to address water pollution and water contamination—the research topics that formed the basis for his Stockholm Water Prize in 2023.[3]

What Does NOT Constitute Evidence?

As part of my job, I get the privilege of listening to people who have spent the better part of their lives researching a particular topic. I suppose I could get similar benefit from watching experts give talks on YouTube (or "You Tub," as I call it). More recently, we had a guest speaker at our business school for an academic debate on stakeholders versus shareholders. Stakeholders are considered any party with an interest or concern in a corporate activity. Shareholders, on the other hand, are the parties that provide capital funds to an organization so it can exist and grow. On this particular evening, the core of the debate was ethics—whether or not publicly traded organizations should be solely focused on the wants and desires of the shareholders or whether there was an imperative to consider all stakeholders, including those not financially invested in the company, to the same extent. The debate was fantastic and it gave me a lot to think about, but it is not the core point I am trying to make.

At the welcome dinner the night before the debate, one of these world-renowned thinkers was talking about his challenges discussing the ethics of corporate activity with individuals who get their information from sources like Facebook, Snapchat, or Instagram. His new phrase in such situations was "you're not even wrong." It took me a while to really get at the meaning of what he was saying, but eventually I realized there is a level below wrong (perhaps outright wrong) when individuals talk about matters without using any systematic evidence at all.

It is not that I am anti-Facebook, -Snapchat, or -Instagram. However, I am reluctant to consider them sources of reliable evidence. Much the same argument can be made from news outlets that are in the business of creating click bait, which is essentially inflammatory and provocative semi-fictional stories to lure people into watching or reading more, with the specific intent of generating advertising revenue. It is so easy to get sucked into this vortex. However, remembering the deficiency of evidence here might just be a way out of this vortex.

What is happening if Facebook, Snapchat, Instagram, or another cherished media outlet becomes your primary source of information? You are anchoring, which is a well-studied cognitive bias. In its simplest form, anchoring is a heavy reliance on the first source of information you find as you think about a topic. For example, you may find yourself too dependent on information posted on Instagram with respect to a political candidate and not spend enough time seeing additional information that is equally critical for understanding that candidate's complete character and position.

A secondary problem may also arise: overcommitment. This is another judgment and decision-making bias, described as a deepening commitment to something even if the outcomes are less desirable. In the preceding political example, imagine you are initially drawn to a Democratic candidate because of something you read on one of your preferred media outlets. Soon after, you have a positive experience with a Republican candidate and start to think about other aspects of politics and policy that are closely aligned with your values. Yet despite your desire to change political groups, you remain with the Democratic candidate. There is nothing wrong with making such a change, but you feel pressure to stay the current path. Your hesitation to change direction is overcommitment.

The Lightning Rod

There are many examples of people who have embodied the notion of evidence-based thinking and talked openly and frankly about contentious topics in society using research evidence. In 2018, I read a book by psychologist Jordan Peterson titled *12 Rules for Life: An Antidote to Chaos*.[4] I enjoyed the book immensely because of the lessons, thoughts, and practical self-help tools the author offers. His dry humor and willingness to be vulnerable are also a nice touch. Little did I know at the time that Dr. Peterson would become a legendary, hot-button debater on topics such as the gender pay gap, capitalism vs. Marxism, white privilege, identity politics, terrorism, the existence of God, and the #MeToo movement. Granted, I may not agree with everything he says, but I do admire his preparedness and his precision of thought. And it is within these qualities of his that I find food for thought.

One particular chapter in *12 Rules for Life* is about being precise with your speech. I am still trying to improve this myself. To me the thrust of this chapter by Dr. Peterson was telling readers to face life straight on with evidence. His message was that the world we live in is harsh and facing those horrors requires a crucial confrontation with evidence.

An example of one of his lightning-rod debates occurred with a BBC interviewer. Dr. Peterson was discussing the gender pay gap, campus protests, and postmodernism. The interview has exceeded forty million views online (not to say that this is the reason I enjoy listening or find it credible). What strikes me as fascinating is his use of evidence-based information in a way that Dr. Denise Rousseau encourages. Dr. Peterson considers the values and concerns of people central to the debate; garners professional opinions; is a master at synthesizing data, facts, and insights about the specific question; and is also rather astute at gathering academic scholarship. There is very little rhetoric in his approach—just evidence. The BBC interviewer wasn't ready for him. Again, it is not that I strongly support his conclusions, I am merely commenting on his use of evidence to inform his thinking.

What I find particularly interesting about Jordan Peterson is that in his debates he openly encourages thinking about tough problems in society through critical appraisal, despite the risk of attack from any number of groups of people. In doing so, even his biggest detractors would have to tip their hat at the number of myths he has debunked and the conversations he has brought to the foreground. It is these conversations that will deeply shape the way we think about our interactions and the world around us.

Can Anyone Engage with Evidence-Based Thinking?

The short answer is, yes. How have I come to know this? When I was finishing grad school, I had the good fortune of working with a business school dean who was highly supportive of case competitions. Even though I had published a few business cases, I was very naïve about what a case competition was.

In short, case competitions are comprised of teams of three or four university students from around the world. These students descend on a university campus to compete for a few days. It is much like the World Cup of rugby or football (the one where players use their feet a lot). There are pools and the winning teams advance to the subsequent rounds. Student teams are given a ten- to twenty-page written case about an organization with a business problem, sent into a closed room for a few hours, and then present to a panel of judges for twenty to thirty minutes (including a question and answer session) on their analysis and recommendations for the organization. Then the winning team is crowned!

Harvard Business School was one of, if not the first, universities to start using cases in the education of business managers. Now many schools deploy this pedagogical approach. Competitions are just a natural evolution of this practice. Many of these business cases competitions involve complex and contextualized decisions.

In my role as the director of this program, I was tasked with establishing and developing a case competition program. I needed a winning model to guarantee continued funding. I quickly realized that these competitions had nearly a complete lack of evidence-based thinking. It was highly frustrating to see a barrage of chaotic presentation approaches with little substance, so I did what any academic would do and turned it into an experiment.

I started with a base of competitive and thoughtful students. We structured each practice session around stakeholder concerns, practitioner judgment and expertise, local data and experimentation, and best available research. Students built playbooks of scholarship on a range of problems, much like a sports team would prepare and craft strategies for approaching different game scenarios. More and more they approached each case problem with a framework for evidence-based thinking that was scalpel-precise.

What happened? They won a disproportionate number of competitions around the world because of their ability to dissect problems and offer evidence-based solutions. They answered judges' questions with grace by summarizing their thinking based on the elements of research, stakeholder concerns, local data, and experimentation. It was extraordinary that such a small case competition program could rack up so many international wins in such a short period. A supportive dean and openminded students using evidence-based thinking was the winning equation! In an academic article I published on this experiment,[5] I closed by suggesting the state of business education is at a crossroads and the sustainability of those we educate in b-schools—those who will go on to make corporate decisions in the future—hinges on teaching this method of thinking.

Why Focus on Quality Evidence?

Evidence-based thinking is not a particularly novel approach to thinking and solving problems. It has been used in medicine and law for many years and is now gaining some traction in business schools around the world. However, it remains underutilized in practice outside these small domains. It is a habit worth forming, so you don't start thinking a 3.7 GPA is the sole measure of a student's worth. Science-informed evidence includes stakeholder concerns, practitioner judgment and expertise, local data and experimentation, and principles derived through formal research. Using this approach will increase the veracity of your thinking.

An informed thinking process is not easy. Let me dispel that now. This is why thirty-second posts on social media offering sweeping commentaries have become so popular: they require little or no thought. Taking your time with decisions requires a framework and process—all of which can be trained. Taking the time with decisions requires us to put our impulsive selves in a timeout (bad Edward, go sit in the corner). Arguing against our anchors, reflecting, seeking insight from experts, understanding stakeholder concerns, and a little local experimentation goes a long way.

 **Practicing the principles of evidence-based decision-making aids with precision of thought.**

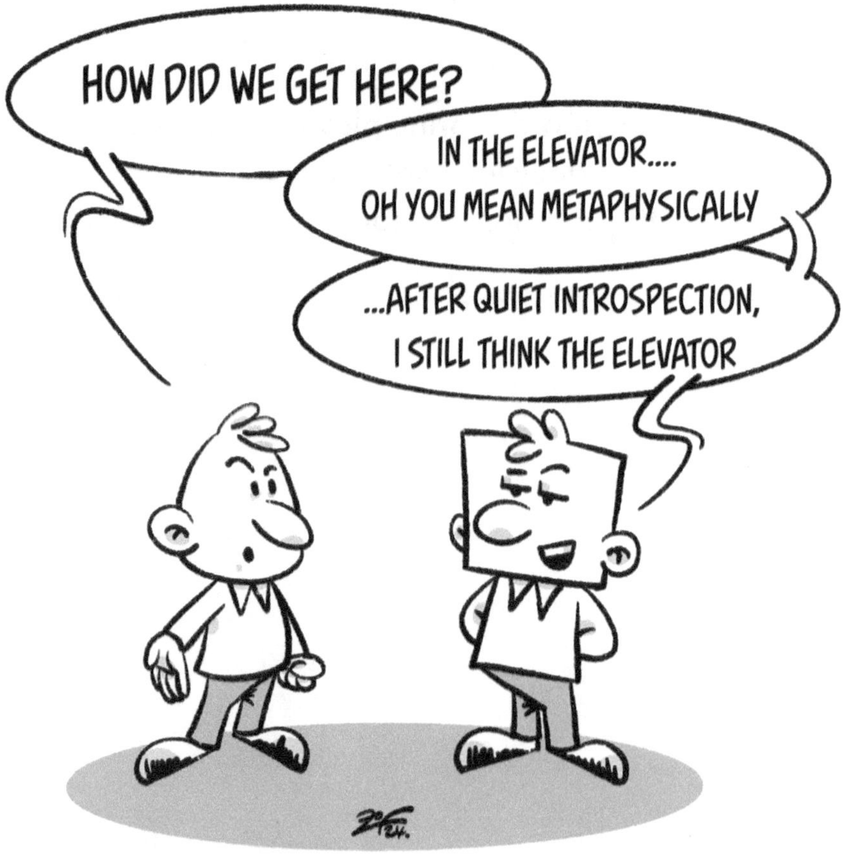
HOW DID WE GET HERE?
IN THE ELEVATOR.... OH YOU MEAN METAPHYSICALLY
...AFTER QUIET INTROSPECTION, I STILL THINK THE ELEVATOR

Chapter Three

Getting in Touch with Your Inner Yoda

> "Whenever you find yourself on the side of the majority, it's time to pause and reflect."
> —Mark Twain

Costa Rica

I've never pretended to be a Spanish-language maestro. I wish I was, but alas, my Spanish skills are about as good as a cat's ballet moves. However, my translation software led me to a nugget of wisdom: "Costa Rica" translates to "Rich Coast." And boy, CR lives up to the hype! Picture a slice of paradise sandwiched between the Caribbean Sea and the Pacific Ocean, home to five million people and a jungle bursting with more fascinating plants and cool animals than one could imagine. My top picks? Sloths, toucans, and howler monkeys. Seriously, who needs Netflix when you have nature's show right in front of you? But maybe my Dr. Seuss view of the Rich Coast has more to do with the bustling pharmaceutical, financial outsourcing, and software development industries within its borders.

The highlight though was surfing. Tamarindo is the place. You see, the main reason for my jaunt was to escape the icy clutches of mountain weather and hang out with old pals on the beach. We all decided to ditch our chilly woes and bask in the Central American sun. Oh, and there was a small matter of a surf camp on the agenda too. Little did I know surfing was less about riding waves and more about embracing the art of falling gracefully. Picture me, a 225-pound, 6'4" human tumbleweed attempting to surf. Spoiler alert: gravity always wins. But hey, I made some spectacular sand angels in the process. I still remember being thrown from a wave trebuchet. What a wild experience!

In my moments of surfboard-induced humility, I found solace in minor improvements. Although some waves had me questioning my choices. After numerous bodily encounters with my surfboard, compounded by a dozen or so sand-plants, and the occasional win, I turned to lounging on the beach, recovering from my surfing antics. As I sat on the beach, watching my friends take a wave beating or two, I overheard a group of people talking about something fascinating: the Blue Zones. To my surprise I heard that Costa Rica was one of the secret spots of long-living folks.

These Blue Zones are like real-life fountains of youth, where people live longer, healthier lives. How? Well, they chow down on plants, move those limbs regularly, enjoy a sip of the good stuff, catch their Zs, and surround themselves with love and laughter. It sounds like a recipe for eternal happiness, doesn't it? But wait, there's more. Knowing these secrets is just the appetizer; the main course is figuring out how to sprinkle these life-enhancing elements into our own routines.

It's all about the application, and the starting point is reflection. After a read of *The Blue Zones*,[1] I had distilled some drops of wisdom. Some regions around the world have nailed it with this style of living. Demographers have identified high concentrations of centenarians in Nicoya, Costa Rica; Okinawa, Japan; Sardinia, Italy; Icaria, Greece; and Loma Linda, California—all of whom embrace these principles for longer living. But then came the hard part, something few do—a heavy dose of reflection.

The secret sauce is reflection. Yup, that's the magical ingredient. Reflecting on our choices, our habits, and our adventures is like polishing the lens through which we see the world. Without reflection, we're stuck in our tunnel vision, like a stubborn goat with blinders. So, this chapter isn't just about sharing the secrets to living a long life (although I think it is helpful). It is about taking information, like the Blue Zones research, and thinking about it in terms of how we can use it to expand our perspectives. This is a friendly nudge to reflect, ponder, and maybe even do a little shimmy of enlightenment.

Who needs a crystal ball when you've got reflection? It's the Jedi mind trick we all need in our lives! By flexing our reflection muscles, we open the door to important insights, and in doing so we also start to close the door of narrow-blinded thinking. Taking the time to think and reflect helps us purge our frustrating, messy, and toxic logics.

Figure 3.1

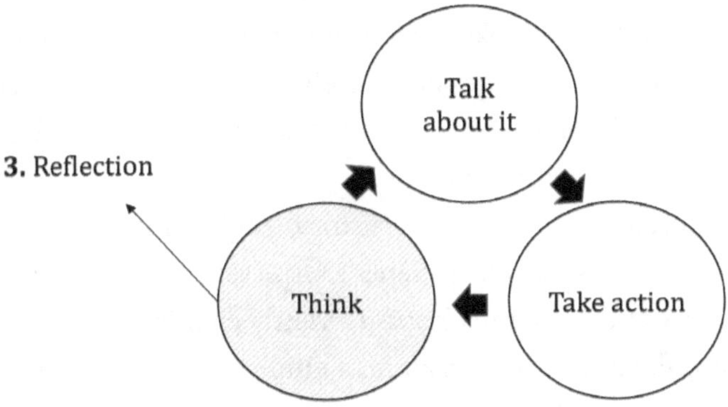

3. Reflection

Talk about it

Think

Take action

Combating narrow-blinded thinking through reflection.

What Is Reflection?

J.K. Rowling's literary masterpiece *Harry Potter and the Goblet of Fire* contains a symbolic description of the art of reflection that reads, "One simply siphons the excess thoughts from one's mind, pours them into the basin, and examines them at one's leisure. It becomes easier to spot patterns and links, you understand, when they are in this form."[2]

Rowling's words not only paint a vivid picture of the reflective process but also unveil the elegant simplicity behind the act of contemplation. This description encapsulates the essence of introspection, that process by which we transform our chaotic stream of consciousness into a tranquil pool of clarity.

While I gravitate toward what I fondly term "Rowling's Reflection Style," where introspection resembles the delicate artistry of pouring thoughts into a basin for careful examination, there are additional definitions of reflection to consider. For instance, the perspective offered by the esteemed minds at the University of Hull in the UK. According to these scholars, reflection involves a multifaceted effort. It encompasses the thoughtful consideration of the learning process—how we acquire knowledge with the intent of enhancing it. It involves a deep contemplation and critical review of specific events or personal aspects, dissecting them with an analytical lens. Moreover, it extends to the construction of theories, where our experiences and observations serve as the building blocks for our unique theoretical frameworks. In this light, reflection emerges not merely as a casual mental exercise but as a deliberate, intellectual endeavor that enriches our understanding and refines our cognitive abilities.[3]

Throughout the annals of history, Stoic philosophers like the luminaries Marcus Aurelius, Seneca, Epictetus, Cato, Zeno, Cleanthes, Hecato, and Musonius Rufus fervently championed the profound merits of reflection. Their wisdom, a guiding light through both tempestuous storms and sunlit serenity, resonates across centuries. When I employ the term "stoic," I refer to a philosophy deeply rooted in the pursuit of unbiased, lucid thinking—a quest to grasp universal virtues such as wisdom, justice, courage, and moderation. These contemplations birthed principles that serve as timeless signposts, illuminating the path for generations to come, regardless of their circumstances.

For instance, the immortal words of Epictetus echo through time, "To make the best of what is in our power, and take the rest as it occurs."[4] This profound maxim encapsulates the essence of stoic reflection, urging us to harness our agency over the controllable aspects of life while serenely accepting the unpredictable twists of fate. In the world of stoicism, reflection emerges not just as a solitary practice but as a beacon, guiding humanity toward enduring tranquility and profound understanding amid life's ever-shifting tides.

But why bother with reflection? It can feel like a daunting mental workout, a labyrinth of biases, a silence too loud, especially when we crave human connection. Facing our own thoughts, or the lack thereof, can be intimidating. Yet, there is a silver lining in this endeavor. When we dive into deep contemplation, exploring territories we might have previously neglected, a world of positive outcomes awaits. It's not just a mental exercise; it's a transformative journey.

Through profound introspection, unexpected treasures surface: heightened self-confidence, mastery over our emotions, sharpened judgment, self-appraisal leading to personal growth, a glimpse into our authentic selves and motivations, the knowledge and confidence to craft our own identity, and perhaps most significantly, the birth of fresh insights. Think of it as sculpting a masterpiece from a block of marble; reflection carves out the intricate contours of our minds, unveiling the extraordinary potential within us. So, despite the initial hesitations, the rewards of this inward odyssey are boundless, promising a richer, more profound understanding of ourselves and the world around us.

How Do You Do It?

Let's face it, we all know people who are quick to pass judgment but rather slow to reflect. Chances are, we probably don't like these people very much. So, how can we avoid falling into this unfortunate trap ourselves? This query was posed to me by one of my graduate students, seeking a concrete process to enhance her reflective abilities. In the moment, I stumbled over my words, responding with a hesitant, "Interesting question . . . I'm not entirely certain, but let me ponder it." After she departed, her question lingered, echoing in my thoughts like a puzzle waiting to be solved. The pursuit of an effective framework for reflection had begun.

Delving deeper into this intriguing inquiry, I examined experiences that I have had over the years while working with extraordinary people. I reflected not only on these personal experiences but also drew inspiration from diverse cultures I'd encountered during my travels. The amalgamation of these experiences helps to shape a practical framework, or rather, a guide for the intricate art of introspection—a roadmap for honing one's reflection skills.

The timing of this student's question was nothing short of serendipitous. At that juncture in my professional journey, I found myself grappling with fundamental inquiries that reverberate in the corridors of academia.

Simultaneously, I found myself interested in the rising tide of young adults who were seemingly offended by a myriad of issues, always the victim. Was I, in my quest for understanding, out of touch with this generational wave, or was this trend of offense by proxy merely a passing fad? My attempts to fathom the depth of these sentiments led me to engage my students in earnest conversations. Yet, the responses I received resembled a complex jigsaw puzzle, a medley of words and phrases borrowed from the media landscape. When I probed further, seeking clarity, I sensed their discomfort, their agitation palpable in the face of my inquiries and logic nudges. I remember asking a student a question about taxes and having another student yell at me, "Dr. Gamble, the rich should pay more than their share of taxes to uphold their end of civil society. That's just the way it has to be!" This marked the inception of a remarkably uncomplicated yet deeply effective method of reflection.

Questions

It all begins with a simple act: asking questions rooted in fundamental logic. Over the years, I have encountered extraordinary individuals hailing from diverse corners of the globe and spanning various professions. What sets these remarkable souls apart is their ability to pose straightforward yet deeply insightful questions. Their curiosity isn't an attempt to showcase intellect, a trait often prevalent in academic circles. Instead, they exude genuine inquisitiveness and a keen interest in others.

Curiously, some tend to associate the art of asking meaningful questions with specific professions. The assumption might be that a high-powered attorney or consultant would naturally possess this trait. However, my experiences have defied this stereotype. I firmly believe there is no direct correlation between one's profession and the ability to ask engaging questions. The key lies in humility and an innate curiosity about the world.

This approach serves as the foundational step in my reflective process (<u>questions</u> → history → principles → meditation → meaning). Yet, regrettably, many individuals never progress to this point. Their lack of interest in others and a preference for the sound of their own voice hinder their potential for genuine reflection.

History

Why delve into the collective wisdom of history? Well, diverse perspectives on history might offer some clarity to this pondering. The philosopher Georg Hegel remarked, albeit somberly, "The only thing we learn from history is that we learn nothing from history."[5] Theodor Reik eloquently mused, "It has been said that history repeats itself. This is perhaps not quite correct; it merely rhymes."[6] And I really appreciate the warning, often attributed to Winston Churchill, that "Those that fail to learn from history are doomed to repeat it." Yikes. If these quotes don't jolt us into a moment of contemplation, I don't know what will. The echoes of our past hold the keys to unlocking a wiser, more enlightened future; it's a lesson worth embracing.

The recent COVID-19 pandemic serves as a stark illustration of the historical lesson I am emphasizing. As the world grappled with the unprecedented challenges posed by this devastating pandemic, numerous questions arose: What would be the fate of humanity amid this crisis? How should we respond? Regrettably, only a handful chose to delve into the annals of history, where the shadows of past pandemics loomed large, offering useful insights waiting to be unearthed.

Throughout history, humanity has weathered deadly plagues, from the relentless onslaught of the Plague of Justinian to the chilling ravages of the Black Death, the New World diseases, smallpox, the Third Plague, influenza, and the menacing emergence of HIV/AIDS. Each of these pandemics tells a story not just of suffering but of resilience, adaptation, and, crucially, lessons learned—like policy, response times, cultural practices that precipitated problems, or the value of science-informed decisions.

By studying these historical pandemics, we could have gleaned invaluable knowledge. How did communities react in the face of despair? What interventions proved effective, and how were societal panic and inequalities quelled, if at all? Understanding the intricate interplay of cultural beliefs and research practices during these times of crisis could have illuminated our path forward.

Remarkably, the answers to these questions were not lost to history; they were present during the COVID-19 pandemic. Yet, tragically, our collective response often lacked the wisdom we could have derived from historical reflection. The opportunity to learn from the triumphs and failures of our ancestors was at our fingertips, but all too often, we chose to disregard these useful insights, leaving us vulnerable to repeating the mistakes of the past. It is a somber reminder of the importance of embracing the wealth of knowledge embedded in our shared history, a knowledge that, if heeded, could guide us toward a more resilient and enlightened future (questions → <u>history</u> → principles → meditation → meaning).

Principles

I've always been averse to drowning in an information deluge. My brain is too small for such vast amounts of information. That's why I've cultivated a habit of synthesizing information, shaping it into guiding principles. In essence, I ask myself, "What might unfold if I focus on a small set of specific principles, practices, norms, or conventions?" This approach serves as a wellspring of knowledge, allowing me to extract the core ideas or lessons.

In my role as a researcher, I've dedicated myself to constructing principles or heuristics through my scholarly pursuits. During a brief stint, I delved into researching nonprofit performance.[7] Fortunately, my earlier explorations into Buddhism and its historical evolution provided a unique perspective for approaching this research. I was particularly fascinated by how Buddhists perceive the world around them and whether this lens could be used to view and measure nonprofits.

This curiosity laid the foundation for a subsequent research paper, where I tried to understand how Buddhist principles—embracing a pro-scientific philosophy, nurturing personal responsibility, practicing healthy detachment, fostering collaboration, and embracing a wholesome worldview—could shed light on the realm of nonprofit performance measurement. These principles, rooted in a profound understanding of human consciousness and values, offered a fresh lens through which to explore how nonprofits could imbue their performance measurement practices with awareness, higher meaning, and connectedness (questions → history → principles → meditation → meaning).

Meditation

Transitioning from principles to the fourth stage of reflection is undeniably challenging. Meditation, in particular, poses a significant hurdle for me. Finding stillness amid today's bustling environment might feel like a monumental task, a battle against time itself. I can empathize—I often find myself wrestling with the clock, struggling to carve out moments for introspection. Yet, taking the time to quiet our minds leads to profound advantages.

In the unhurried stillness of quietude is where breakthrough awaits. Despite the initial resistance, the practice of meditation is akin to mining gems from the depths of our consciousness. In fact, a study exploring mindfulness meditation revealed compelling outcomes.[8] Individuals with extensive meditation experience demonstrated heightened emotional intelligence, along with reduced perceived stress and enhanced mental well-being, compared to those who practiced meditation less frequently or not at all.[9] These findings merely scratch the surface; a plethora of documented health benefits further underscores the powerful potential of this practice. A brief scan of the research through Google Scholar will demonstrate this point.

To me, meditation serves as a conduit, allowing us to connect and apply learned principles in our endeavor to decipher the bewildering complexity of the world. It's a deliberate act of stepping back, immersing ourselves in the sanctuary of quiet contemplation, and emerging with newfound clarity and understanding amid life's craziness (questions → history → principles → meditation → meaning).

Meaning

At its core, this entire process of reflection culminates in the pursuit of meaning—an attempt to rationalize our thoughts and find coherence amid complexity. Yet, many rush to this final stage, adopting absolute positions with unwavering certainty. These rigid stances can be exasperating, and they all too easily creep into our minds. To combat the tendency, employing a continuum approach, as opposed to an absolute approach, can be invaluable.

A continuum approach, whereby our stances and beliefs fall on a spectrum, is a manner of crafting a multidimensional map of our convictions. Picture taking two opposing or seemingly unrelated concepts and placing them on a continuum, with an intricate grid of possibilities stretching in between. Whether it's religion, the definition of family, environmental perspectives, job classifications, tolerance for adversity, or governmental policies—each can find its place on this spectrum. For instance, the continuum for religion might range from "no God" to "one absolute God," while environmental concerns could span from "no global warming change" to "severe global warming."

When you look at initially disparate ideas simply as different points along a continuum, neat combinations reveal subtle nuances, offering intriguing alternative insights and unraveling the intricate web of reasons behind our beliefs. It is within these intersections that profound meaning flourishes.

From my perspective, meaning is where gaps emerge, new paths unfold, identities and practices reform, thoughts realign, and connections with others deepen. It's a realm where we comprehend our relevance in the broader context, learn to convey clearer messages, and perhaps even invite joy and serendipity (karma) into our lives. Ultimately, it's in this process of exploring the interplay of ideas that we cultivate not just understanding, but a richer, more meaningful existence (questions → history → principles → meditation → meaning).

Does the Practice of Reflection Really Yield Practical Benefits?

From my experience, I would answer with a resounding yes. A modern-day example of stoic reflection is neuroscientist and philosopher Sam Harris. Dr. Harris earned a PhD in cognitive neuroscience from UCLA. He embodies the multidisciplinary essence of neuroscience, integrating fields like physiology, anatomy, psychology, physics, computer science, math, chemistry, molecular biology, and developmental biology. In his philosophical works, he seamlessly intertwines the roles of master reflector and scientist.

What sets neuroscience apart from other disciplines is its holistic approach to understanding humanity and the world. Driven by the pursuit of balanced and fulfilled living, Harris delves into profound topics in his books and meditation practices, exploring philosophy, rationality, and religion. Moreover, he shares his passion with listeners in a compelling podcast, where he endeavors to unravel the complexities of the mind and society. From examining the enigma of happiness to dissecting the components of a meaningful life, from analyzing the divisiveness of America to contemplating the future of plagues and artificial intelligence and pondering the depths of consciousness, Harris fearlessly delves into intricate subjects.

While these topics might initially appear daunting, Harris possesses a remarkable ability to reflect and elegantly convey tricky concepts on big topics like purpose and meaning. His dedication to understanding human nature and the world serves as a beacon, inspiring us all to embrace reflection as a means to navigate the complexities of our existence.

Another exemplar of the profound power of reflection is Viktor Frankl, the esteemed Austrian psychiatrist who pioneered logotherapy, a philosophy centered on the search for meaning in one's life. Frankl's unique perspective is deeply rooted in his harrowing experiences as a prisoner in various Nazi concentration camps, providing an unparalleled depth to his insights. His ability to delve into both the existential and humanistic dimensions of existence, particularly within the context of World War II concentration camps, is nothing short of awe-inspiring.

Frankl's groundbreaking hypothesis, borne from his time in the camps, posits that an individual's vision of their future directly correlated with their likelihood of survival in such dire circumstances. This insight not only underscores the significance of hope but also illuminates the profound impact of reflection on one's resilience and longevity.[10] Moreover, Frankl transcends his personal ordeal, emphasizing the universal importance of collective reflection—an endeavor that seeks to comprehend life's meaning from myriad perspectives, not confined to a singular viewpoint. He suggests that this was critical for him during some horrific times in his life. His enduring legacy resonates as a testament to the power of reflection, urging us to explore life's complexities from diverse angles, thus enriching our understanding of the human experience.

The wisdom encapsulated in a Buddhist quote illustrates the transformative power of introspection: "Since everything is a reflection of our minds, everything can be changed by our minds." This sentiment finds remarkable resonance in the teachings of the current Dalai Lama, the spiritual leader of the Tibetan people. His Holiness stands as a living symbol of reflection, gazing both backward and forward in time through a multitude of lenses.

Delving into the depths of the human psyche, the Dalai Lama exhibits a remarkable concern for inner exploration, urging us to scrutinize the very essence of happiness within our minds. His teachings encourage cultivating harmony among diverse religious traditions, emphasizing the universality of spiritual values that bind humanity together.

Central to his philosophy is the nurturing of trust, hope, and mental resilience through transformative practices like meditation and reflection. In a world often marred by negativity, the Dalai Lama's timeless wisdom shines brightly. His classic one-liners, such as "anger is bad for our health," serve as poignant reminders of the interconnectedness of emotional well-being and physical health.

Moreover, his insight into the transient nature of human existence is encapsulated in his wise words, "We are all here on this planet as tourists . . . so while we are here, we should try to have a good heart and make something positive and useful of our lives." This profound call to action echoes the essence of reflection, inspiring us to contemplate our purpose, nurture kindness within, and contribute positively to the world around us.

Walking on a Trail

During my recent visit home to Canada for Christmas, I found solace in the paradoxical beauty of my hometown. The landscape was festooned with chemical plants that, during the festive season, transform into magnificent structures resembling giant Christmas trees, despite their actual identity as petrochemical factories. Amid this industrial spectacle, there existed a serene sanctuary—a sprawling rail trail enveloped by majestic trees, stretching for miles.

One crisp winter day, I embarked on a solitary walk along this trail, the ground beneath me dusted lightly with snow. As I strolled, I found myself introspecting, reflecting back on the past year. Alone with my thoughts, I posed crucial questions to myself. I can't remember if I spoke them aloud or just asked questions quietly to myself. I am sure if it was the prior, I would have scared any other walkers off the trail. As I pondered my accomplishments and areas for improvement, I contemplated the historical patterns I aimed to break and the valuable principles I had gleaned on my personal journey. In the midst of nature, I distilled the year into a few buckets of importance. For the next hour, I immersed myself entirely in these reflections. Surprisingly, the process left me both mentally drained and euphorically elated.

What I found most revelatory was this: why was it this exercise of self-reflection only occurred annually, at the year's end or in between my surfboard beatings (a.k.a. "surfing lessons")? The realization became my key takeaway. I recognized the true potency of introspection lay in its regularity. The joy and fulfillment I experienced could be amplified if I practiced it more frequently—not merely on a yearly basis, but on a monthly, weekly, even daily cadence. The transformative power of consistent self-reflection dawned on me, urging me to envision a state where this practice became an integral part of my routine.

The potential for combating narrow-blinded thinking and contempt through personal growth, collective understanding, and positive change is boundless, waiting to be unlocked through the simple yet profound act of introspection.

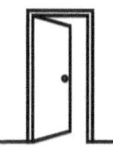

Reflecting can drastically improve clarity of thinking.

TALK ABOUT IT!

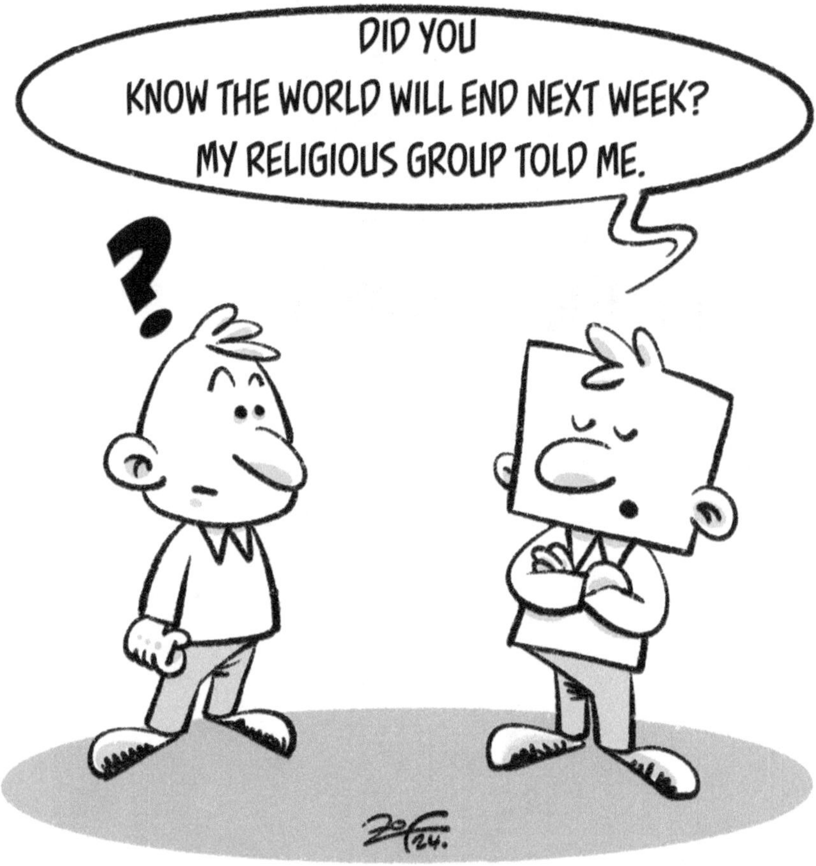
DID YOU
KNOW THE WORLD WILL END NEXT WEEK?
MY RELIGIOUS GROUP TOLD ME.

Chapter Four

Group Blinders

"For it is dangerous to attach one's self to the crowd in front, and so long as each one of us is more willing to trust another than to judge for himself, we never show any judgement in the matter of living, but always a blind trust, and a mistake that has been passed on from hand to hand finally involves us and works our destruction. It is the example of other people that is our undoing; let us merely separate ourselves from the crowd, and we shall be made whole. But as it is, the populace, defending its own iniquity, pits itself against reason. And so we see the same thing happening that happens at the elections, where, when the fickle breeze of popular favour has shifted, the very same persons who chose the praetors wonder that those praetors were chosen."

—Lucius Annaeus Seneca

The Blue Kool-Aid

In the colorful era of the 1950s, the Kool-Aid Man strutted onto screens and pages, a sugary cherry drink personified. Armed with his signature catchphrase "Oh, yeah," he burst through walls, aiming to charm his way into every kid's heart. And boy, did he succeed! Kool-Aid™ became an instant hit, an icon of sugary delight for little ones (and maybe some adults, too).

Little did the Kraft ad wizards know their beloved mascot would unwittingly pave the way for the dark idiom "drinking the Kool-Aid." The sad and infamous Jonestown Massacre was a chilling chapter of history in which hundreds who'd fallen prey to a murderous cult led by Jim Jones knowingly drank a poisonous elixir of cyanide mixed in a similar (but not the same) sugary drink. This innocent phrase would later become synonymous with buying into a bad idea.

Cults, as it turns out, are as diverse as the beverage aisle in our grocery store. From the innocuous to the sinister, they span a broad continuum. Full disclosure, I hail from a customary Irish Catholic clan, complete with Sunday church visits. I attended church school, not so much for divine enlightenment, but in pursuit of the post-church Tim Hortons donuts. Looking back, my upbringing, while seemingly innocuous, could fall under the umbrella of a "cult," as per the Oxford Dictionary definition of one as "a system of religious veneration and devotion directed toward a particular figure or object."[1] However, it's not just religious circles that harbor cultish tendencies. Cults can emerge anywhere, rooted in a misplaced or excessive admiration for a person or thing.

So, as we sip our Kool-Aid and munch on our donuts, let's remember that cults also come in myriad flavors—some sweet and harmless, others disturbingly bitter. The lesson? Be cautious about what you're sipping and who's serving it!

Religious Groups

In retrospect, my experiences as an altar boy who was fired for my penchant for passing out (apparently due to some sort of medical thing), and my expulsion from St. Peter's Basilica in Vatican City for the mere crime of bare knees, signaled perhaps the conventional religious path wasn't precisely my calling. Chris D'Elia's comedic dissection of the quirks of Catholicism, especially our bemusement when priests engage in scandalous acts, provides both laughter and a sobering reflection on the faith.[2]

His recounting of revisiting church as an adult, armed with his "made up adult brain," struck a chord. The surreal act of pretending to consume a symbolic body and blood like a vampire, punctuated by inexplicable chants and declarations, left me chuckling endlessly. Yes, I grasp the symbolism, but Chris's humorous perspective resonates deeply, "forever and ever." Don't get me wrong; I did glean positive values from my church days. Virtues flourished in those architecturally beautiful buildings; however, we cannot ignore the detritus and duplicity interwoven within religious structures either.

It wasn't until my stint in Australia, teaching economics at a fervently religious private school, that my theological curiosity was piqued. My seemingly benevolent employers would occasionally let slip comments that raised eyebrows ("How many times have you praised God today, Edward?"). Rather than dismissing these not-so-subtle nudges, I set out on a religious exploratory expedition, attending services from Assembly of God, where tongues were spoken, to exploring Pentecostalism, Mormonism, Hari Krishna, and more. Each faith system clung to their beliefs, guided by spiritual leaders whose interpretations were viewed as mystical truisms.

During my inquiries, I asked spiritual leaders and followers alike about the reasoning behind their practices. Many times, their responses were vague, the histories unclear. I questioned the prominence of their prophets, inviting uncomfortable silences. When I dared to push back on their logic, I was met with defensiveness. But I must say, some of my experiences at these places of worship were bolstered by exceptional music, others by great food, and some by magnificent architecture (which they do not pay property tax on . . . tsk tsk).

Asking questions and challenging dogmas has led me on an interesting theological journey. A striking pattern emerged in my conversations with people of various religious groups: when confronted with questions about their practices and history, or criticisms, their responses often wavered. A fog of vague explanations and silences enveloped these discussions. In moments of candor, individuals admitted a sense of superiority, dismissing other groups as "not the chosen ones." It appeared that everyone sought cleansing and salvation, myself included.

Most intriguing was the collective certainty among these groups. Each believed they were right, and the rest were unequivocally wrong. Their singular-tracked conviction illuminated the dangers of groupthink for me. When I stripped away the "who" part of the deity in question, the patterns and practices were staggeringly similar. Many attendees were born into the religion of their "choice."

Yet, amid the dogma, I discovered a universal truth: The essence of community lay in faith beyond oneself. That faith serves as the adhesive that binds communities together. Buddhism (often not considered a religion, per se) notably stood out, emphasizing scientific philosophy, personal responsibility, detachment, collaboration, and a wholesome worldview.[3] It was a revelation.

Strikingly, most religious groups share this trait. Ironically, their shared conviction in being unequivocally right highlights the peril of groupthink. This realization underscored the importance of individuals who courageously challenge their own faith communities, disrupting the echo chamber of unwavering beliefs. Their courage fosters growth within the rigid doctrines, reminding us that even amid the deepest beliefs, talking about beliefs is an essential, liberating act.

For example, a recent investigation by CBC Fifth Estate shed light on such courage.[4] A Canadian Mormon dared to question the transfer of $1 billion of tithing funds to Brigham Young University in the US, sparking controversy within his own community and questions of duplicitous behavior shrouded in religious self-rightness. His act of defiance against accepted norms within the Church, despite dismissals, highlighted the need for scrutiny, not just within religious institutions but also from regulatory bodies like the Canada Revenue Agency.

The point is that the danger of groupthink is palpable. To escape this stifling conformity and combat narrow-blinded thinking and contempt, it's imperative to engage in conversations with groups holding alternative beliefs. It's through these dialogues that we crack open the first fissures in the fortress of rigid beliefs.

Figure 4.1

Talk about it
1. The dark side of groupthink
Think
Take action

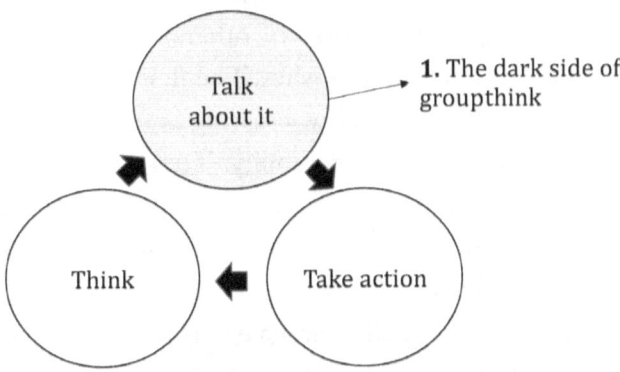

Combating narrow-blinded thinking by challenging groupthink through discussion.

Is Groupthink Synonymous with Don't Think?

To explore this concept, let's delve into the intriguing interplay between the words "groupie" and "groupthink." First, consider the notion of a groupie—an informal term denoting individuals ardently following someone famous, often displaying uncritical enthusiasm. I am imagining a Metallica concert in Toronto, where eager fans would go to great lengths to catch the attention of James Hetfield.

This enthusiasm, however, becomes the breeding ground for groupthink—a phenomenon of irrational and potentially perilous decision-making rooted in the desire for conformity and harmony within a group. It's a scenario where individuals agree with each other not out of genuine consensus, but to maintain a façade of unity (or out of fear).

As aptly put by William Whyte Jr. of *Fortune*, groupthink manifests as "a rationalized conformity—an open, articulate philosophy which holds that group values are not only expedient but right and good as well."[5] This tendency toward conformity can be disastrous, leading to catastrophic outcomes in historical events like Pearl Harbor, the Vietnam War, and the Bay of Pigs invasion, as meticulously analyzed by psychologist Irving Janis.[6] Simply put, in these situations people didn't speak up to challenge the prevailing group view despite holding some doubts or objections, and then bad things happened.

Janis's research (and the works of others) unveils three distinct devices by which groupthink flourishes. The first is an overestimation of the group's power and morality, creating an atmosphere of blind optimism—an illusion of invulnerability. The second arena fosters closed-mindedness, where individuals rationalize their ideas while stereotyping those outside their group, dismissing them as unintelligent or irrelevant. It is an "us versus them" mentality that further entrenches groupthink. The third arena exerts pressure for uniformity, stifling dissent and encouraging self-censorship. Those who challenge or deviate from the group narrative are labeled as disloyal, effectively suppressing diverse perspectives.

Weak or False?

The heart of the matter lies in the false sense of cohesion groupthink provides, pushing individuals to conform, even at the cost of critical thinking. It becomes a perilous cycle, where genuine dialogue and dissent are stifled in favor of an illusionary harmony. It raises a pressing question: In the face of groupthink's dangers, how do we foster genuine conversation and critical thought within our communities?

In the academic scholarship around the topic, there are valuable insights on the wreckage caused by groupthink. The work of Jonathan Haidt, for instance, provides a thought-provoking perspective on group dynamics. Haidt delves into the intricate mechanisms that reinforce group behavior, notably shedding light on our penchant for faultfinding within other groups.[7]

In his book *The Happiness Hypothesis*, Haidt aptly observes the allure of scandal, emphasizing how it provides a unique and comfortably passive form of entertainment. He writes, "Scandal is great entertainment because it allows people to feel contempt, a moral emotion that gives the feeling of moral superiority [over another or another group] while asking nothing in return. With contempt, you don't need to right the wrong (as with anger) or flee the scene (as with fear or disgust)."[8] In other words, scandal lets us feel good about ourselves while cutting down others, all while demanding no action of us to rectify perceived wrongs.

Haidt's exploration of destructive group moralism and the divisive nature of group self-righteousness resonates deeply. It illuminates the inherent peril that lies within such group behavior, serving as a stark reminder of the harm it can inflict on both individuals and society at large. As we navigate the intricacies of group dynamics, Haidt's insights compel us to reevaluate our own roles and responsibilities in countering the dangers of groupthink.

Category Problem

Ah, the deceptive world of categories! It all starts innocently enough—grocery stores neatly sorting food into frozen, fresh, pantry, fruit and vegetables, meat, and dairy. But oh boy, when these categories extend to sports teams, races, religions, and political affiliations, things get spicy!

Categories are the Pandora's boxes of groupthink. They seem harmless, a way to define who's who and what's what. They help us communicate the group's essence, their deeds, and why they matter. It's all fine until someone starts wielding categories like a blunt instrument, excluding or overlooking crucial details. It's like when you're passionately arguing with your friend about whether a tomato is a fruit or vegetable—trust me, it can get heated! Is this how spicy salsa got invented?

Here's where it gets tricky. False categories, much like the tomato debate, can lead to epic misfires. They blind us, making us miss out on brilliant solutions because we're too busy toeing the line of the dominant group paradigm. And that is how we end up with misalignment failures. In the grand scheme of life, arguing over whether a tomato is a fruit or vegetable is amusing, but imagine doing the same with serious matters. That's where things go haywire in political discourse.

So, the next time you're tempted to label something or someone, remember the tomato conundrum. Be aware of the pitfalls of groupthink lurking in those categories. After all, nobody wants to be the person arguing over tomatoes while missing the bigger, juicier picture!

Where Might I Be Wrong?

Finding the balance between meaningful group (or category) dynamics, such as fostering a sense of belonging and personal growth, and blind adherence to a singular truth, exemplified by extreme actions dictated by indoctrinating leaders, is crucial. Darwin's concept of cohesion sheds light on this balance. Consider a rowing team in which each member competes individually to secure a spot, yet they must unite cohesively as a team to beat their competitors. This scenario illustrates both ingroup and outgroup dynamics simultaneously. In this and similar scenarios, natural selection operates on multiple levels, urging individuals to contemplate their group dynamics critically and acknowledge potential flaws in their discussions. Without recognizing these nuanced layers of ingroup and outgroup dynamics, genuine conversations cannot occur. The key lies in understanding these complexities to foster meaningful dialogue and genuine understanding within groups.

Developing the skill to combat groupthink is a valuable practice demanding conscious effort. Personally, I've discovered an effective question that prompts me to contemplate the perils of groupthink: Where might I be wrong? This question, rooted in counterfactual thinking, encourages me to explore perspectives divergent from the prevailing conversational consensus.

Counterfactual thinking, despite its name suggesting opposition to facts, serves as a gateway to mapping alternative ideas, challenging the prevailing group mentality. Let's term this approach "counter-group" thinking. In the realms of both research and everyday decision-making, embracing alternative explanations and fresh perspectives is essential for a well-rounded decision set. It is through thoughtful inquiry and open discussion that we can actively nurture the habit of considering counter-group thinking, fostering a more nuanced and robust understanding of the topics at hand.

Let me illustrate the concept of counter-group perspectives through a tangible example. Across various sectors, organizations often seek certifications to convey their adherence to specific standards or ethical practices, such as certified organic or certified fair trade. However, I encountered a distinct certification called B Corporation Certification through a friend who founded a manufacturing organization in the Western region of the US. B Corp status, administered by B Lab,[9] signifies a commitment to a wide swath of social and environmental missions. Notable companies like Patagonia and Ben & Jerry's proudly hold this certification.

Despite widespread assertions that obtaining B Corp certification leads to revenue growth, I found myself met with resistance when I questioned the empirical basis for this claim. B Corp enthusiasts dismissed my inquiries, viewing my skepticism as an affront to their collective belief that doing good inevitably translates into financial success. Undeterred, I embarked on a rigorous three-year data collection project, engaging in deep conversations with B Corp–certified executives and meticulously gathering financial data, primarily from privately held North American certified B Corps.

My co-authors and I made a groundbreaking discovery. Our research revealed a counter-group insight: B Corp certification was actually associated with a short-term growth slowdown, particularly pronounced among smaller and newer firms. The explanation we offered for this was managerial attention issues, but the finding challenges the prevailing narrative, shedding light on a nuanced aspect of the certification's impact that is often overlooked. By delving into the complexities of real-world data and engaging directly with

B Corp–certified organizations, we unearthed valuable insights that broaden our understanding of the relationship between social responsibility and financial performance.[10]

However, before I pat myself on the back for successfully applying counter-group alternatives, I must recount another experience where I failed to heed my own advice. A close friend and I were conducting a research project delving into ski resorts' environmental engagement strategies and reporting processes.[11] Some might dismiss this endeavor as a mere indulgence, given my passion for skiing, but I assure you it was far from the case. As we prepared to engage with the CEOs and CFOs of various ski resorts, I was insistent with my co-researcher and close buddy Gary that our questions should revolve around the pressing issues of global warming and climate change. I assumed these executives, given their industry's reliance on the environment, would undeniably share my concerns. My simplistic assumption was that rising temperatures would lead to less snowfall and more rain, rendering outdoor snow skiing impossible. However, Gary wisely cautioned me to pause and consider an alternative or counter perspective that challenged my preconceived notions.

As it turned out, Gary was right (which he often is). Several ski executives presented a far more nuanced view, arguing the dynamics of snowfall were intricately complex. They emphasized that attributing temperature swings solely to global warming and climate change oversimplified the issue. The experience highlighted a crucial lesson for me about the importance of engaging in conversations with diverse groups and listening to the collective expertise and lived experiences, especially when looking at an industry with which I was not intimately familiar.

This encounter reinforced how crucial it is to remain open-minded and receptive to alternative viewpoints through discussion. It served as a reminder that genuine understanding arises from dialogue underpinned by a willingness to challenge our own assumptions, leading to a richer and more comprehensive grasp of complex topics.

Embracing counter-group insights, indulging in counterfactual thinking, or simply considering the contrary perspective all circle back to a fundamental question: Where might I (or you) be wrong? Getting in the habit of asking yourself this question in conversation, in research, and in life isn't just a tool; it's your secret weapon in the battle against narrow-blinded thinking and contempt, adding a dash of humility to every discussion.

Feel the Krak and Wit

It's often taken for granted, but engaging in meaningful dialogue, particularly within the framework of the "where might I be wrong" philosophy, demands an active effort to listen and consider the counter perspectives of others. A prime example of someone adept at exploring these contrary viewpoints is the acclaimed American author Jon Krakauer. His nonfiction works, in particular, have left a lasting impression on me. One standout piece is *Under the Banner of Heaven*,[12] a meticulously researched exploration of the shadowy aspects of extreme Mormonism and the evolution of the Church of Jesus Christ of Latter-Day Saints (LDS Church).

In this gripping account, Krakauer delves deep into the history of Mormonism, unraveling the complexities surrounding figures like Joseph Smith, the contentious criminal fraud trial he faced, the practice of polygamy, the persecutions endured, and the subsequent rise of Brigham Young.

For someone like me who is intrigued by diversity of religious beliefs, Krakauer's approach to presenting these counter perspectives proved incredibly insightful. By immersing myself in the counter-narrative, I gained a broader and more nuanced understanding of the LDS Church in terms of its historical context, its contemporary manifestations, and its extreme factions. Krakauer's ability to navigate these intricacies not only enhanced my knowledge but also reinforced the importance of embracing diverse viewpoints to form a comprehensive and enlightened worldview.

In his compelling work *Missoula*,[13] Jon Krakauer once again demonstrated his prowess in presenting thought-provoking counter perspectives. While millions of Americans indulge in their weekly dose of college or professional football games, Krakauer dared to offer an alternative viewpoint. Set against the picturesque backdrop of Missoula, Montana, Krakauer painted a stark and unsettling portrait of the prevalent rape culture within the University of Montana, particularly involving the football team. What makes the narrative all the more disturbing is the university's failure to address these issues judiciously and effectively.

Krakauer, along with other astute observers, contends this unsettling reality may not be confined to Missoula alone, but is a pervasive failing of numerous university institutions. The insatiable drive to have a winning football team, increase student enrollment, and build a formidable brand often comes at an unimaginable cost. *Missoula* challenges us to confront the uncomfortable truth that beneath the glitz and glamour of college sports and institutional prestige lies a disturbing underbelly of misconduct, exploitation, and injustice.

By shedding light on this disconcerting counter perspective, Krakauer prompts us to delve deeper into the institutional fabric of our society. He encourages us to reevaluate the priorities of our educational institutions and question the moral dilemmas arising from the relentless pursuit of athletic excellence and institutional fame. The unsettling questions raised by Krakauer's exploration serve as a clarion call for further examination, urging us to confront the harsh realities that often lurk behind the façade of success and achievement. In doing so, *Missoula* becomes not just a book, but a powerful catalyst for societal introspection and change, encouraging us to ask, "Where might we be wrong?"

Admittedly, one of my all-time favorite comedians is the brilliantly witty Ricky Gervais. Gervais possesses a unique talent for injecting humor even into the glitzy world of the Golden Globe Awards, which he has hosted on multiple occasions. At this grand spectacle celebrating international excellence in film and television, where stars strut in their glamorous outfits and accolades flow like champagne, Gervais gives an alternative perspective. The quintessential English comedian, actor, writer, and director, Gervais marches in armed with his razor-sharp wit and irreverent humor to challenge the dogmas of the industry.

What sets Ricky apart and what I absolutely appreciate in his hosting style, is that he doesn't just bask in the glory of Hollywood's successes; oh no, he fearlessly delves into the murky waters, exposing Tinseltown's underbelly, poking fun at its quirks, eccentricities, and downright misgivings with a comedic finesse that leaves the audience in stitches. I mean, this man has hosted the Golden Globe Awards not once, not twice, but a whopping five times! That's five rounds of Hollywood roasting, each time more hilarious and daring than the last.

And it's not just about the laughs; Ricky's genius lies in his ability to offer a counter perspective, to remind us that even Hollywood's most powerful A-listers should make room for another reality. Take for example this one:

Apple roared into the TV game with *The Morning Show*, a superb drama about the importance of dignity and doing the right thing—made by a company that runs sweatshops in China. You say you're woke, but the companies you work for, I mean, unbelievable: Apple, Amazon, Disney. If ISIS started a streaming service, you'd call your agent, wouldn't you? So if you do win an award tonight, don't use it as a platform to make a political speech, right? You're in no position to lecture the public about anything. You know nothing about the real world. Most of you spent less time in school than Greta Thunberg. So if you win, come up, accept your little award, thank your agent and your God, and f**k off.[14]

Harsh, yes, but an alternative perspective worth considering.

Our Collective Dogmas

The perplexing conundrum of "in" and "out" group dynamics is the place where the line between camaraderie and chaos is thinner than a strand of spaghetti. Imagine you're happily strolling through the landscape of social connections and networks, reveling in the delightful company of your group. Life is good, you think, until suddenly, you find yourself hurtling headfirst into what I call the "Kenny Loggins Danger Zone"—that treacherous territory where group cohesion morphs into fanaticism and extremism faster than you can say "groupthink."

Here is an example of challenging dogma I recently faced with my friend Rick, over the intricacies of property tax in Vermont. Now, don't get me wrong; I firmly believe in the importance of households, businesses, and nonprofits paying their fair share of land tax. After all, property taxes serve as a vital financial backbone for our communities, funding essential services like firefighting, police protection, education, arts and entertainment, community fitness initiatives, and the maintenance of parks and roads.

However, my curiosity led me to a troubling realization. What happens when the hard-earned land tax dollars of a community are siphoned away, leaving the area bereft of crucial resources?

This was the very real dilemma I sought to unravel in Vermont. Astonishingly, around 80 percent of land tax revenues in many Vermont communities are diverted elsewhere to fund education, leaving the state with one of the highest property tax rates in the entire US. I couldn't help but wonder, does this practice truly foster community growth and better educational outcomes?

In my pursuit of answers, I engaged in conversations with various groups despite encountering a fair share of hostility. Amid the passionate discussions, I discovered a pivotal moment in Vermont's history—the Vermont Supreme Court's decision in the *Brigham vs. State of Vermont* case, which deemed the then-existing educational funding system unconstitutional. The landmark ruling birthed Act 60 (1997), a legislative effort aimed at achieving a fair balance of educational spending across school districts. It was, in essence, a modern-day Robin Hood narrative. Take from the wealthy and distribute resources to the rural communities—but with very little accountability.

Curiosity piqued, I delved deeper into the mechanics of how property tax was calculated, seeking insights from town assessors. To my dismay, there seemed to be a lack of clarity and understanding regarding this process, despite its pivotal role in determining taxable amounts. Furthermore, I probed the rationale behind the substantial reallocation of funds—80 percent, in some cases—to rural education. Interestingly, I found that this decision, rooted in various acts, was contentious, and though many disagreed with its interpretation, they remained silent.

As I examined the educational outcomes resulting from the significant reallocation of tax dollars, my findings were disheartening—there appeared to be no discernible improvement. This led me to a groupthink insight: even though most Vermont residents did not understand the backdrop of their property tax, virtually no one challenged the prevailing view. They just wrote their property tax check every year. There was no pushback, and limited feelings of tax sovereignty.

What do you do if you've entered a parallel universe where open-mindedness has gone on an extended vacation and ignorance is the new tour guide? When you find yourself in a group that frowns upon dissenting opinions faster than a toddler rejects vegetables, it's time to channel your inner Maverick. Consider it your social duty to seek out another person or, better yet, another group—one that welcomes diverse viewpoints like a hungry diner welcomes a buffet spread. Break free from the shackles of groupthink! It can happen on any matter.

Take measures against the perils of groupthink by engaging in "counter-group" conversations and by asking, "Where might I be wrong?"

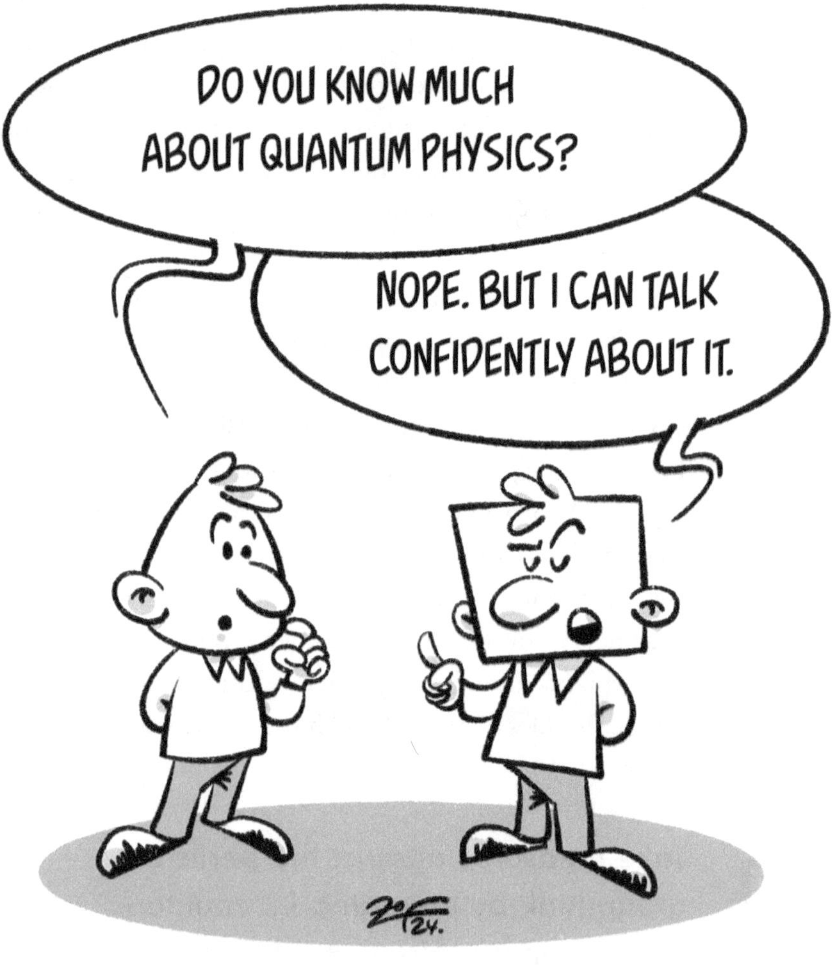
DO YOU KNOW MUCH ABOUT QUANTUM PHYSICS?
NOPE. BUT I CAN TALK CONFIDENTLY ABOUT IT.

Chapter Five

Shaking Off Overconfidence

"Overconfidence will drown you in the sea of reality."
—**Unknown**

The Infection of Overestimation

Nestled at the crossroads of Uganda, the Democratic Republic of Congo, and Rwanda lies a mesmerizing region adorned with untamed jungles, awe-inspiring mountains, and vibrant national parks—a paradise for nature enthusiasts and adventure seekers alike. During one of my research excursions, I seized the opportunity to embark on a personal dream to see the majestic mountain gorillas in their natural habitat. Little did I know this decision would lead me to an impactful and unforgettable experience now etched forever in my memory.

In a lush valley I was enveloped in the dense foliage of the wild where every rustle of leaves and distant calls of exotic birds create a symphony of nature. Armed with a machete, I ventured forth, determined to witness the magic of this wilderness at its depths. As I walked, families of gorillas emerged, their dark eyes curious yet cautious, observing my presence from a short distance. The air buzzed with energy as infant gorillas, brimming with curiosity, played around, their innocent gazes locking onto mine, as if seeking to unravel the mysteries of the human world.

What struck me the most was the palpable sense of community among these majestic creatures. Parents, with watchful eyes, gently reprimanded their playful offspring when they ventured too close, showcasing a deep understanding of the familial bonds that transcended species. And then there were the colossal silverback males, their imposing presence magnified by their broad chests and muscular arms, weighing an impressive 300–350 pounds. Despite the initial fear that gripped me as I stood a mere 10 meters away, I couldn't help but marvel at their regal demeanor and awe-inspiring strength.

It was a dance of fear and fascination, an intricate interplay of primal instincts and profound admiration. Standing in the presence of these giants, I felt an overwhelming sense of humility, realizing that I was merely a guest in their world. The sheer majesty of these gorillas, with their human-like features and sophisticated social behaviors, left an indelible mark on me.

In those moments, I was not just an observer; I was a part of something much larger, a participant in the heart of the African wilderness. The experience was a reminder of the delicate balance between humanity and nature, a testament to the wonders awaiting those who dare to venture beyond the familiar, and an enduring lesson in the art of coexistence with the natural world. As I left that enchanted place, I carried with me not just memories but a weighty sense of gratitude for the opportunity to witness the untamed beauty of the gorillas, a treasure that will forever enrich my understanding of the world we share.

During my expedition deep into the heart of the jungle, I was also confronted with a harsh reality which shook me to the core. The mountain gorilla, a majestic and awe-inspiring creature, stands perilously close to extinction. In that moment, I believed their endangerment was primarily due to the encroachment of human activities on their habitat—their territory cleared for farming, their homes razed for fuelwood. However, my African guides shared the chilling truth with me of the multifaceted threats these magnificent beings face.

I learned that gorillas often fall victim to hunting snares set for other animals, a cruel twist of fate highlighting the collateral damage of human greed. Moreover, the illegal trade in gorilla parts, driven by the insidious motive of financial gain, further imperils these giants. The very essence of their existence, their lives, and their lineage are being ruthlessly exploited, pushing them to the brink of extinction.

As I absorbed this heartbreaking information, I delved deeper, hungering for a better understanding of the intricate web of challenges that surround the survival of the mountain gorillas. The guides, with a mixture of sorrow and determination in their eyes, painted a vivid picture of the intertwined struggles faced by both the gorillas and the local inhabitants in these parts. Their narratives told of communities ravaged by hunger, plagued by disease, and torn apart by unrest, their dire circumstances mirroring the plight of the endangered gorillas.

In the quiet moments of the evening, I found myself in deep contemplation, moved by these experiences. The emotional impact of my trek through the forest and the encounter with these magnificent creatures was overwhelming. On the one hand, I was filled with awe, utterly mesmerized by the experience of witnessing these majestic beings up close. It was as though I was peering into a mirror—not in the literal sense (I am not 350 pounds, hairy, or muscular) but in a figurative way. The gorillas' actions, such as delicately picking up a plant between forefinger and opposable thumb and consuming it just meters away from where I stood, seemed surreal. Their eyes, deep and soulful, locked onto mine, making time stand still.

Yet, this sense of wonder was marred by a contrasting wave of anger. I couldn't shake the intense frustration I felt toward my fellow humans in the region who displayed such coldness and hostility toward the gorillas. The very creatures I had just witnessed in all their splendor were being endangered by human activities—farming, clearcutting, and poaching—all driven by an insatiable desire for financial gain. The realization struck me with a bitter truth: the root of the problem lay in the relentless human pursuit of survival and wealth. It brought to mind a poignant comment from one of my close friends who once said, "Humans are the meanest species on the planet." This harsh reality served as a stark reminder of our species' capacity for destruction, even in the face of such natural beauty and magnificence.

In those reflective moments, my emotions were a tumultuous blend of wonder and anger, mixed with a profound sense of responsibility. The dichotomy of the gentle giants before me and the harshness of human actions weighed heavily on my heart, compelling me to confront the darker aspects of our nature. It ignited a resolve within me to advocate for change, to raise awareness, and to foster empathy, hoping that through collective efforts we can alter the course of this narrative and ensure the survival of these extraordinary creatures for generations to come.

In retrospect, I cringe at my initial arrogance. How naïve I was to believe I held the key to solving the complex issues plaguing the region. Fortunately, I managed to keep these presumptions to myself, sparing both the locals and the staff at my accommodations from having to hear of my misguided overconfidence. It dawned on me how many well-meaning visitors to remote parts of the world might fall into the trap of assuming they know what's best, speaking from a Western perspective without truly understanding the intricacies of the situation.

I had been guilty of that very arrogance, confidently asserting my opinions after just a few days in the area, despite my limited knowledge. In my overzealousness, I believed I possessed the perfect solution to the problems at hand. I was convinced my analysis was flawless and my viewpoint unquestionably correct.

The peril of overconfidence became abundantly clear. How swiftly we sometimes make uninformed comments, lacking the caution, humility, and respect to recognize our own limitations. However, reality hit me hard. After shedding my initial misguided confidence, engaging in candid conversations with the locals, and investing countless hours in learning about the issues impacting them, my perspective underwent an important transformation. I delved deep into the local dynamics, looking at food security, conservation practices, government policies, energy and economic development plans, and cultural traditions. What emerged was an array of intricacies, emphasizing the delicate balance of the ecosystem of which the gorillas were an integral part. More importantly, it showed me that I needed to learn more (or at a minimum just park my absolutism).

The pivotal lesson here lies in recognizing the genuine danger of overconfidence. It stands in the way of what might otherwise be fruitful conversations. To shake off this self-imposed constraint, humility, and a genuine willingness to learn, are indispensable. By recognizing our limitations, approaching discussions with an open mind, and embracing opportunities to absorb knowledge through conversations with those intimately connected to the issues, we can temper our egos and reach a more realistic sense of how much we do and don't know. In doing so, we pave the way for truly productive and meaningful dialogues that foster understanding, empathy, and collaborative solutions. The end of narrow-blindedness and contempt is around the corner! One task is to unmask the illusions of omniscience.

Figure 5.1

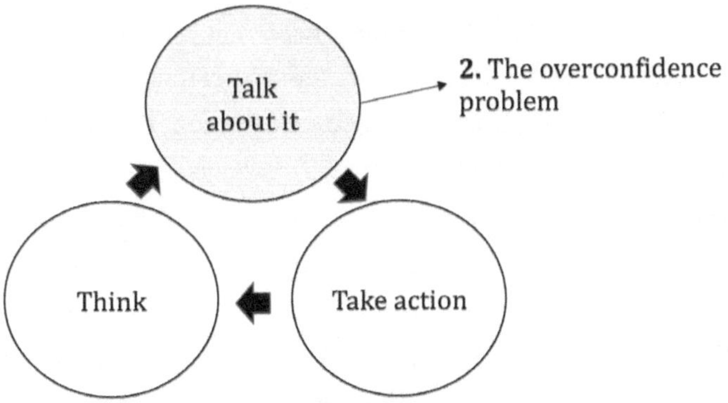

Combating narrow-blinded thinking by reducing overconfidence.

Overconfidence Unveiled

Prepare to be amazed by the revelations of Daniel Kahneman and other experts, which show that in the vast landscape of psychological and economic research, biases stand out as intriguing distortions of reality. These biases, whether in estimating events, gauging our accuracy, or ranking things, often shape our decisions more than we realize. Renowned expert Daniel Kahneman sheds light on one of the most compelling biases: overconfidence.[1]

Overconfidence is a fascinating phenomenon, showcasing our tendency to misjudge or miscalibrate the probabilities of subjective outcomes. In other words, because of our strong convictions, our perceptions of what did or what will happen often diverge significantly from reality. This intriguing bias manifests in at least three distinct ways. First, there's overconfidence in our performance, where we tend to believe we performed better in a given activity, job, or interaction than we actually did. Second, there's overplacement, wherein we overestimate ourselves compared to others, even when the reality paints a different picture. Finally, there's overprecision, or our unwavering certainty in the accuracy of our beliefs, views, or opinions, even when they might be far from the truth. These three facets of overconfidence reveal the intricacies of human perception and shed light on the intriguing distortions that shape our understanding of the world.

We have all witnessed these phenomena. Edward, feeling overly confident about his culinary skills, decides to host a dinner party for his friends, despite having limited experience in the kitchen. He announces that a gourmet three-course meal will be prepared. Ignoring recipes and culinary advice, Edward's "feast to remember" is better forgotten for good reasons. As the night unfolds, he miscalculated timing in the kitchen and never got around to making an appetizer. His main course, intended to be a masterpiece, ends up overcooked and smelling like a hint of a wet dog. And his fancy dessert turns into a sticky mess. Hilarious instances of overconfidence like this happen every day.

Chapter Five: Shaking Off Overconfidence

In the annals of history, there are powerful real-world instances where overconfidence spiraled into catastrophic outcomes, vividly illustrating my point. Tragically, unwarranted confidence has played a significant role in several devastating incidents. Consider the Chernobyl disaster, where overconfident employees overlooked crucial safety measures, resulting in a nuclear meltdown and a staggering casualty count exceeding 4,000, as reported by the World Health Organization.[2] The *Titanic*'s crew famously believed the ship was unsinkable, a notion shattered when more than 1,500 lives were lost at sea.[3] Similarly, the Space Shuttle *Columbia* disaster might have been averted had unchecked overconfidence not clouded decision-makers' judgment. In the aftermath, debates emerged, suggesting that the dismissal of damage indicators by the Debris Assessment Team, driven by overconfidence, played a role in the catastrophe.[4] Furthermore, the BP oil spill in the Gulf of Mexico stands as a glaring testament to the dangers of overconfidence. Rig operators, contractors, and even government entities, in their overconfident stance, contributed to the release of hundreds of millions of gallons of oil. This disaster incurred a colossal fine of $18.7 billion for BP.[5] These sobering examples underscore the dire consequences that can arise when overconfidence blinds us to the risks at hand.

While many examples of overconfidence might seem distant, it didn't take me long to recall instances from my own life. A particularly memorable one occurred while skiing with a friend in the backcountry of Montana. It's safe to say that he and I don't make the best skiing duo, both of us having been afflicted by the curse of overconfidence on skis. Together, we share an inexplicable belief that launching ourselves off cliffs is a brilliant idea, as if we possess the skiing prowess of professional athletes. It's remarkable how easy it is to get caught up in the "I can do anything" mindset, even when facing potential risks. Thankfully there were no broken legs that day, but there were abundant face plants, plenty of bruises, and a sobering snow slide or two. Our overconfidence even got us dangerously close to the precipices of a few cliffs with unwanted endings.

Reflecting on these experiences, I can't help but contemplate the impact and importance of parking our overconfidence. What if we made a habit of pressing pause to reconsider our unwavering beliefs, views, and knowledge? What if, instead of jumping headfirst into situations fueled by overconfidence, we took a moment to discuss the nuances and assumptions? Perhaps, by doing so, the distortions in our thinking might become clearer, thus paving the way for more informed decisions and a deeper, more accurate understanding of the world around us.

Who Needs Humility? I Am an Expert!

Daniel Kahneman, in his enlightening book *Thinking, Fast and Slow*, delves into the intricate world of human biases, including the captivating realm of overconfidence.[6] One of the intriguing facets he explores is the art of snap decision-making among "experts," emphasizing that quick judgments are often a product of a lifetime's worth of experiences. However, even these seasoned individuals are not immune to occasional blunders, reminding us that errors are inevitable, regardless of expertise.

You have to admit it's a comedic spectacle when novices believe they can bypass the accumulation of deep knowledge and experience and become instant decision-making wizards just by reading a couple books or tuning into a few podcasts. It is, then, truly fascinating to me when I encounter the rare breed of seasoned experts who take the time to dissect patterns and reflect before adopting a stance on topical matters. Allow me to introduce you to two unsuspecting examples of this wisdom.

When I first considered people like Tony Robbins and Admiral William McRaven, I instinctively associated them with extreme overconfidence. Their remarkable achievements and influential status seem to let them naturally exude confidence. But upon closer inspection, I realized what sets them apart isn't overconfidence but rather a profound humility.

Tony Robbins, the charismatic motivational speaker, is often seen as the epitome of confidence. His journey from a challenging upbringing to becoming a billionaire, best-selling author, self-help guru, and mentor to the stars might suggest overconfidence. However, delving into his books reveals a unique humility. Robbins actively seeks knowledge, asking questions of experts in a genuinely humble manner. He openly admits what he doesn't know and actively searches for answers. Through his writings and talks, he shares his deep belief in the value of learning and synthesizes his findings to help others, such as in his book *Money: Master the Game*.[7] He not only learns from the best investors but also extends his wisdom by offering a comprehensive game plan for anyone interested. Moreover, he practices what he preaches, contributing to society through his foundation for the young and homeless.

Similarly, the legendary Navy SEALs, synonymous with hyper-confidence, reveal a different truth upon closer examination. Admiral McRaven, a four-star admiral with extensive combat experience, embodies confidence without veering into overconfidence. His speeches and book, *Make Your Bed*,[8] illustrate a man who has engaged deeply in conversation and reflection. He imparts invaluable life lessons, emphasizing the significance of the little things, inner resiliency, embracing failure, seeking guidance, demonstrating leadership during adversity, and the power of discipline. His approach isn't about mere confidence; it's about understanding the complexities of life through continuous dialogue and introspection.

What strikes me about both Robbins and McRaven is their willingness to remain open, embracing conversations and reflections before solidifying their positions. Behind their confident exteriors lies a foundation of humility, a trait often overshadowed by their accomplishments. Their willingness to engage in multiple iterations of discussions, to distill core principles, and then share their insights confidently gives us the ultimate model for open-mindedness and reflective wisdom. This blend of confidence and humility, far removed from overconfidence, distinguishes them as extraordinary leaders who are truly curious and nonjudgmental.

Grounded

Remember in Chapter 1 when I described the academic debates my graduate students engage in as part of their coursework? These lively exchanges are head-to-head, evidence-informed competitions in which students argue for or against a singular proposition, such as "tax-exempt nonprofits should pay property tax." What I didn't delve into earlier were some of the unintended, yet incredibly positive, consequences of these debates.

Many students approached me afterward to share their experiences. I would often hear a polite knock on my office door, and a student who had participated in the debate that day or that week would pop their head in to say something along the lines of, "Professor Gamble, thank you for making us do the debate. It was stressful and demanded more preparation than I anticipated. But I am genuinely glad I took part. I feel proud of myself; it was truly beneficial because I learned how to dial down my overconfident views and listen to the person sitting across from me."

For a vast majority of students, a remarkable outcome of these debate experiences was the transformation in their perspectives. Overly confident bravado in their initial approach turned into calm and engaging dialogue and debate with their peers in later rounds. Their convictions softened and, in some cases, their perspective on a topic completely changed through debate. Witnessing this shift in perspective was nothing short of astonishing. It showcased the power of discourse and critical thinking, highlighting the ability of well-structured debates to challenge preconceived notions and foster intellectual growth among students.

Overconfidence and entrenched views are not limited to students; they are pervasive issues in society. Consider the topic of taxes, a subject on which many would happily share their "expert" opinion. The reality is that tax evasion in the US has significant consequences for our daily lives. When individuals evade taxes, they erode the tax base, disrupt tax revenue, and undermine federal programs like Social Security and Medicare. Tax evasion directly affects local infrastructure such as roads and community services. Simply put, taxes are the lifeblood of government, society, and our economy.

How do you dig deeper into topics like tax evasion before you comment? I vividly recall a fascinating conversation I had with a gig worker back in 2019, which shed light on the complex issue of tax compliance within this emerging workforce. Gig workers, individuals who earn some or all of their income through online platforms like Uber, Lyft, DoorDash, Care.com, TaskRabbit, and Upwork, operate as independent contractors or freelance workers. At that time, the media was abuzz with news articles and opinion columns expressing concerns about tax noncompliance among gig workers. Estimates suggested the gig workforce in the US had surged to around 60 million people, sparking debates about the minimal reporting, compliance, and payment of federal and state income taxes, as well as self-employment taxes.

This situation interested me because I didn't know anything about it. I do believe in the principle of everyone paying their fair share of taxes, although defining what constitutes a "fair share" can certainly be a subject of debate. Nevertheless, the lack of accountability among gig workers regarding tax payments prompted me to reflect. Initially, my frustration led me down a path of overconfidence, questioning whether these workers were merely being sneaky or whether gig employment inherently attracted a disproportionate number of self-serving individuals. My train of thought spiraled, and I found myself grappling with the enormity of the problem—a significant economic impact amounting to approximately $455 billion.

I decided to embrace the wisdom of curbing my overconfidence and adopting a curiosity-driven and conversational approach to the question. With the assistance of a few colleagues, I embarked on a research jaunt, aiming to talk with gig workers to understand the question of tax noncompliance. As we listened to the insights from these workers, I was astonished by what we discovered. Unlike employees in traditional organizations or those with more established business contracts, gig workers do not always get a W-2 form reporting their income. In addition, gig workers reported heightened levels of uncertainty, stress, and emotional turmoil in their jobs and lives. Together these logistical, emotional, and psychological factors cause underreporting to the Internal Revenue Service. What I initially perceived as a blatant disregard for tax obligations turned out to be a deeply rooted emotional response, painting a far more nuanced picture of the challenges faced by gig workers in navigating the realm of taxation.

Crimson Overconfidence

Is it possible that many, if not all of us occasionally overestimate our performance, place, and precision? The answer is likely yes. The question then becomes, how do we counteract this tendency that significantly adds to narrow-blindedness? The solution, which is surprisingly simple, lies in the art of asking questions and engaging in meaningful conversations.

Since my time in the jungle with the gorillas, I've endeavored to cultivate curiosity before forming opinions, especially when my initial inclination is to react swiftly and confidently. This approach has not only provided unexpected benefits but also led to intriguing conversations. When people are encouraged to share their views, there's an innate desire to listen and be heard. This desire is evident on both sides, even in discussions about contentious topics.

Consider an experience I had in the Netherlands, where my wife and I accidently strolled through the De Wallen region of Amsterdam, a central hub for various adult-themed establishments. Initially taken aback, I later asked a local friend, Lau, about the legality of the situation. The blatant placement was baffling to me, but my ignorance signaled a need for caution and humility. Lau explained the Dutch government had decriminalized prostitution over the past two decades, aiming to empower workers, reduce crime, and enhance labor conditions.[9] Intrigued, I delved deeper into government websites, finding additional evidence for this rationale.

Similarly, Canada has adopted comparable strategies, legalizing small quantities of hard drugs and establishing safe injection sites in British Columbia. The logic behind such actions centers on yielding more positive outcomes rather than criminalizing certain behaviors.[10] While I'm still no expert on these matters, my curiosity led me to explore this perspective, which reduced my initial shock and overconfidence on the matters.

The point is not about fully agreeing or disagreeing with these two approaches to societal and economic problems, but rather understanding the merit in exploring alternative solutions. Julia Child's wisdom resonates here: "You'll never know everything about anything." By approaching discussions with an open mind and withholding premature overconfident judgments, we open ourselves to the power of curiosity, enriching our understanding and fostering empathy in the process.

Dig deeper by engaging in meaningful conversations, with caution and humility, to reduce the pull of overconfidence.

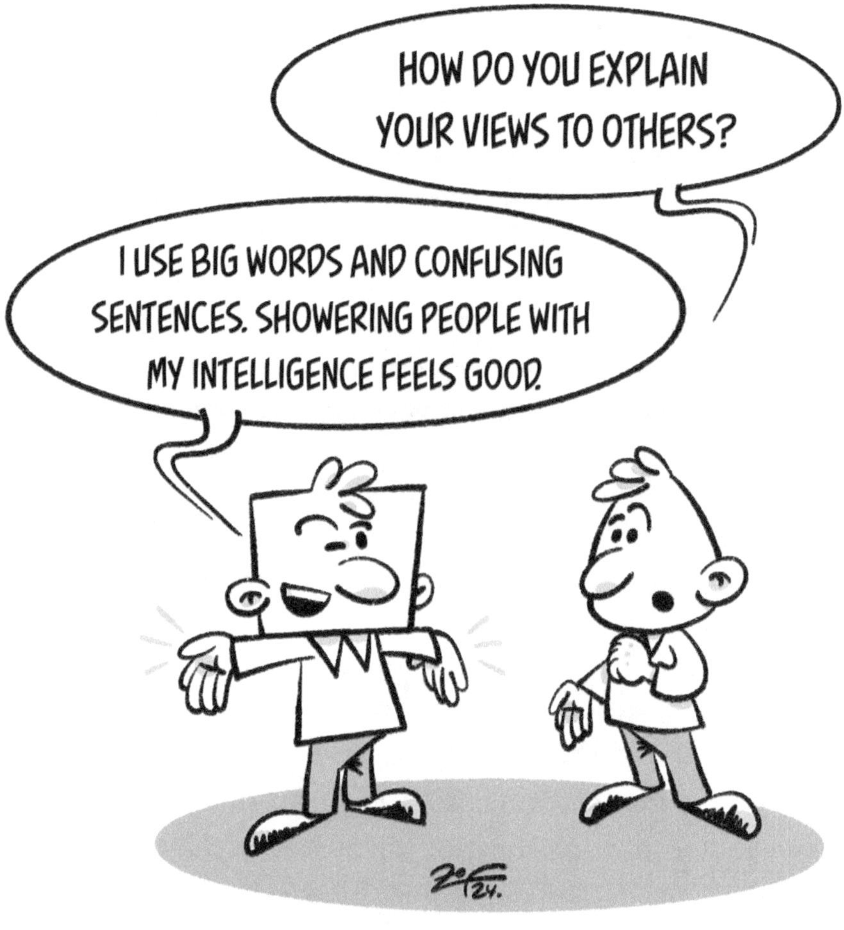
HOW DO YOU EXPLAIN YOUR VIEWS TO OTHERS?
I USE BIG WORDS AND CONFUSING SENTENCES. SHOWERING PEOPLE WITH MY INTELLIGENCE FEELS GOOD.

Chapter Six

The Power of Effective Explanation

"If you can't explain it simply, you don't understand it well enough."
—Albert Einstein

Six Thousand Islands and One Common Tongue

After completing my undergraduate studies in Canada, I found myself yearning for an adventure abroad. Eager to explore the world and broaden my horizons before jumping into graduate school, I embarked on a quest to find the "perfect" destination. With no specific country in mind, I was largely motivated by the goal of immersing myself in a vastly different culture. Having previously lived and worked in various European countries, I ruled out another European escapade. So one evening with friends at a local pub, I sought their input on potential countries for my next adventure. Amid the laughter and camaraderie, one friend casually suggested Japan.

His reasoning was compelling in its simplicity. He spoke of Japan's intriguing allure, its reputation for low crime rates, and its captivating historical heritage. What struck a chord with me, however, was the humorous mental image he drew of a tall Caucasian like me trying to navigate the bustling streets of a sprawling Japanese city. The thought of blending in and standing out simultaneously appealed to my sense of adventure (and my sense of humor). With this whimsical notion in mind, I was convinced Japan was the perfect destination for my upcoming jaunt.

Emboldened by my friend's suggestion, I wasted no time. The very next day, I eagerly began researching job opportunities in Japan, envisioning myself amid the vibrant, alluring world of Japanese culture. The Land of the Rising Sun beckoned, and within a few short months, I found myself boarding a plane bound for Tokyo, my heart brimming with anticipation and curiosity. Little did I know this spontaneous decision would mark the beginning of an extraordinary chapter in my life, filled with cultural discoveries, unexpected challenges, and transformative experiences.

My year in Japan unfolded as a thrilling odyssey, an exhilarating adventure that left an indelible mark on my mind. Immersed in the heart of this enchanting country, I underwent a journey of discovery that transcended the boundaries of my otherwise routine life. I thought the purchase of a motorcycle would be a decision that promised both freedom and excitement. However, fate had other plans, and a daring ride ended abruptly when I crashed headfirst into a wall, leading to an unexpected visit to a rural hospital. Despite the mishap, this incident became a learning moment, teaching me resilience and the importance of embracing both the highs and lows of life's adventures.

Throughout my time in Japan, I became a wanderer, tracing the footsteps of ancient civilizations as I explored historic sites. I indulged in the therapeutic embrace of *onsens*, finding solace in the healing waters and serenity of these natural hot springs. Every meal became a culinary delight, with each dish presenting a tantalizing fusion of flavors and textures, offering a gastronomic experience beyond compare. Wandering through bustling markets and city centers in random cities, I absorbed the vibrant energy of Japanese life, engaging with locals, sampling exotic delicacies, and immersing myself in the rhythm of daily existence.

Beyond the urban sprawl, I ventured into nature's embrace, climbing majestic mountains. At night, I found peace on tranquil beaches, their sands serving as my bed beneath the starlit sky. Along the way, I encountered many remarkable individuals with deep philosophical insights to share on meaning and purpose. These conversations deepened my appreciation for the Japanese people, illuminated diverse perspectives, and broadened my understanding of the world. These interactions also opened my young eyes to the rich cultural nuances—the art of tea pouring and the artistry in Japanese calligraphy. In only a year I developed a foundation and connection with Japan, leaving me with a sense of belonging in a foreign land.

Reflecting on this transformative year, I realized the lessons I absorbed were far more impactful than much of my undergraduate study. The experiences I had in Japan shaped my character, enhanced my resilience, and nurtured my curiosity. As I traversed the landscapes and cultures, I discovered the immeasurable wealth hidden within the realm of human connection and experiential learning.

In the bustling life I led in Japan, a significant milestone emerged—an immersion into the intricacies of the Japanese language. Through dedicated efforts, I attained some level of proficiency, enabling me not only to engage in conversations but also to read and write with some basic fluency. Yet, beyond the grammar and vocabulary laid out in structured lessons and textbooks lay a fascinating realm of real-world communication, rich in nuances and subtleties. This dimension, which I came to recognize as the unteachable essence of how people in a culture communicate, is uncharted by conventional study guides. It comprises an intricate network of deeply embedded characteristics within the act of articulation and explanation.

Living amid the vibrant Japanese culture provided an invaluable education in these unspoken intricacies. It was here I delved into the multilayered art of explaining, understanding that mere words were insufficient to encapsulate the depth of human expression. The journey of learning Japanese was not merely a process of vocabulary acquisition; it was a profound exploration of cultural intricacies, social norms, and the unspoken language of facial expressions—a nuanced negotiation that transcended linguistic boundaries.

When I conversed with someone in Japan, grasping the essence of communication became a multifaceted endeavor, akin to navigating an autobahn, where the flow of ideas and emotions raced at unparalleled speeds. Conversations were not just exchanges of words; they were intricate dances, where we as individuals grappled with our unique cultural perceptions, translating thoughts from Japanese to English and back again in our minds. Each interaction became a delicate balance—a collaborative effort to convey personal perspectives while intricately deciphering the intentions, tone, and explanations of others.

My time in Japan illuminated the vital importance of refining our ability to explain ourselves—a skill I recognized as an art form in constant evolution. The power of explaining our position is a great tool for opening new routes and critical for reducing narrow-blinded thinking and contempt. Through these experiences, I grasped the significance of embracing key principles in communication, transforming mere dialogue into a harmonious collaboration. While I have not mastered this art, the journey of improvement became a source of immense satisfaction for me, a testament to the enduring beauty of human connection and the limitless depths of understanding that lie within the art of explanation. As Fredrik Backman said, "Everything is complicated if no one explains it to you [clearly]."[1]

Figure 6.1

Talk
about it
3. Clarity in
explanation
Think
Take action

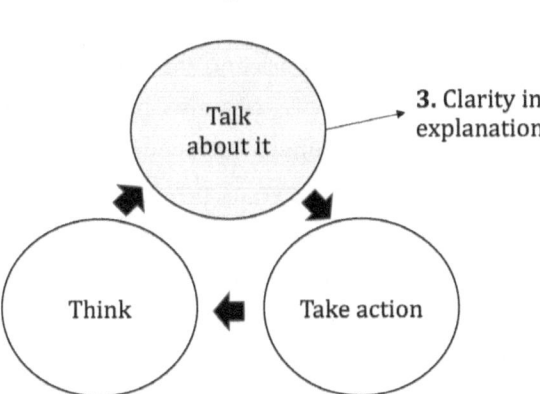

Combating narrow-blinded thinking requires clear and effective explanations.

Why Is Explaining Something So Difficult?

The challenge of articulating our thoughts and emotions is a universal struggle, one that often perplexes even the most introspective minds. While developmental psychologists give a list of reasons for this, I am inclined to adopt a more rudimentary perspective—one rooted in the realm of self-awareness and contemplation, or the thinking that comes before we open our mouths. In our struggle to explain ourselves, we often lack clarity about our own beliefs and positions on various matters. In my view, it is not necessarily an internal blockage that hinders our communication but rather the possibility that we have not delved deep enough into our thoughts.

In essence, our inability to articulate our perspectives may arise from the simple fact that we have not engaged in sufficient introspection. We have not taken the time to contemplate our perspectives, listen to the subtle signals emanating from our subconscious, or respond to the gentle nudges guiding us in our daily lives. This lack of self-awareness creates a mental vagueness, hindering our ability to express ourselves with confidence and coherence.

Drawing inspiration from the field of behavioral economics, I find the intriguing concepts of signals[2] and nudges[3] to be a critical part of this conversation. These subtle cues and influences play a pivotal role not only in shaping our behavior but also in enhancing our ability to communicate effectively. Behavioral economists argue that these signals and small nudges can serve as powerful tools for conveying information, especially in the context of interpersonal communication. By being attuned to them, individuals can gain insights into their own beliefs, enabling them to articulate their thoughts more clearly and convincingly.

Consider the impact of nudges—subtle prompts that steer our actions in specific directions—to recycle, to not litter, to choose to be an organ donor. These nudges, when harnessed effectively, can motivate desired behaviors and, intriguingly, enhance the explanation process. By recognizing the influence of these nudges, individuals can navigate the complexities of communication with newfound confidence, ensuring their expressions are not only articulate but also aligned with their true beliefs.

In essence, the art of explanation starts with understanding the intricate interplay between self-reflection, awareness of subtle cues, and responsiveness to nudges. By embracing these elements, individuals can overcome any struggles they have with self-expression and engage in meaningful conversations that are not only eloquent but also deeply authentic.

When we engage in conversations to explain concepts or ideas, there are crucial elements, often referred to as "signals," that play a pivotal role in effective communication. These signals constitute the context within which explanations are constructed and interpreted, and involve three fundamental components: the signaler, the receiver, and the environment.[4]

The signaler—the person conveying the message—holds a significant responsibility. Listeners instinctively evaluate the signaler's credibility, using it to assess the honesty of the explanation. The quality of the signal, or its reliability, is another crucial aspect listeners scrutinize. Supportable evidence and observability strengthen the signal, making it more convincing. Additionally, listeners assess whether the explanation aligns with their own perspectives (structure or alignment), and they seek consistency and logical coherence (focus) in the information presented.

On the receiver's end, two factors come into play when interpreting signals. First, the listener's level of alertness, or receiver attention, profoundly influences their ability to absorb and comprehend the message. Second, listeners calibrate the incoming signal against their expectations, which shape their interpretation of the explanation (receiver interpretation).

Furthermore, the environment in which the communication occurs significantly impacts both the effectiveness of the signal and the receiver's interpretation. Countersignals, which refer to reinforcing feedback from the signaler, can enhance the impact of the message. Conversely, distortion or noise, indicating non-reinforcing feedback from the signaler, introduces complexities and challenges into the communication process.

In essence, every time we attempt to explain something, we are contending with all three of these factors. Acknowledging the interplay between the signaler, the receiver, and the environment provides valuable insights into the art of explanation. By being cognizant of these elements, communicators can refine their skills, ensuring their messages are not only clear and coherent but also resonate effectively with their audience. Mastering the nuances of these signals empowers individuals to navigate the complexities of communication while fostering genuine understanding and connection in the process.

Framing

The task of explaining something clearly and effectively might feel overwhelming, due to the multitude of signals influencing the process.

However, there's a helpful way to conceptualize this complexity. Over time, the messages or explanations derived from these signals are mentally organized into "frames."[5] These frames are akin to storage boxes, helping individuals process and interpret incoming information by fitting it into preexisting cognitive structures. Picture these frames as mental templates that help people make sense of the world around them.

The concept of framing is pivotal. Imagine these frames as organized compartments within the mind, each representing a specific category or perspective. When an individual encounters new information, they do not create an entirely new mental reality from scratch. Instead, they rely on these preexisting cognitive frames to fit this new information into their understanding of the world. Humans instinctively detect patterns and cues in their surroundings, which their minds then compress, reflect upon, and neatly organize within these frames of reference. These frames imbue the information with meaning, allowing individuals to interpret the world in a way that aligns with their existing knowledge and experiences.

In essence, framing serves as a cognitive tool to help individuals navigate the complexities of incoming information. By categorizing and organizing new knowledge within familiar mental frameworks, people can understand, interpret, and respond to explanations more effectively. Recognizing the role of framing in our thought processes sheds light on how humans construct meaning from the world, demonstrating the intricate interplay between perception, cognition, and understanding.

Numerous studies have underscored the profound impact of framing on decision-making. It's well understood that how a decision is described or framed can significantly influence the choices people make, even in situations where the stakes remain identical. For instance, a compelling study delved into consumer behavior concerning payment methods and found that the framing of the price can dramatically alter their preferred method of payment.

In a study, participants were given a scenario involving a product priced at $1.00, and they could pay using either cash or a credit card.[6] However, the manner in which the price was presented had a remarkable effect on their choices. If the price was framed as $1.00 USD and a surcharge of $0.03 USD was added for credit card transactions, a distinct preference emerged. Conversely, when the price was framed as $1.03 USD with a discount of $0.03 USD for cash payments, a different choice became apparent. The subtle alteration in framing led to divergent outcomes. The mere presentation of the information, whether as a surcharge or a discount, wielded considerable influence over individuals' decisions. This example emphasizes the importance of understanding cognitive biases and perceptual tendencies when analyzing choices, offering valuable insights into the realm of behavioral economics and consumer psychology. It also vividly demonstrates how the framing of an idea or concept can shape our responses in conversations.

Three Ways to Apply Frames in Conversations

How about we shift gears away from these hardcore research examples to delve into more enjoyable and approachable territory? I'm not suggesting we unravel the profound mysteries of cat videos, but I am offering some approaches to add to your explanation tool kit.

There are three distinct approaches to explaining information: mechanistic, reasons-based, and storytelling. Mechanistic explanations delineate causal links, providing a step-by-step account of how A leads to B, B leads to C, and so forth. Reasons-based explanations focus on factual or reasoning aspects, emphasizing the "whys" behind something. Storytelling, on the other hand, revolves around narratives that evoke emotions in a manner that draws the listeners in.

Let's apply these concepts in practice. Consider three diverse approaches to explaining climate change. Now, I must confess, claiming expertise on climate change would be a far stretch from the truth. However, these examples serve as valuable illustrations of the mechanistic, reasons-based, and storytelling approaches to explanation.

Mechanistic Explanation. Numerous scientific studies have established that since 1900, the air temperature on Earth has risen almost 2 degrees. These studies explain that when humans burn fossil fuels, it causes the Earth's temperature to rise. Burning fossil fuels produces carbon dioxide, a heat-trapping gas, which when released into the atmosphere increases Earth's air temperature. One of the biggest causes of carbon dioxide is vehicles with large, inefficient engines. Vehicle carbon dioxide emissions increase the Earth's air temperature as well as the temperature of the oceans, which leads to global changes in precipitation, snow and ice melt, and extreme weather, such as heavy rains, heat waves, and severe storms.

Reasons-Based Explanation. The Earth is our home and we should take care of it. If temperatures continue to rise, the sea level will continue to rise, flooding areas where many people in the United States and around the world live. Outdoor air pollution is likely to increase, which shortens people's lives. In addition, higher temperatures lead to drought and more crop failures. In this way, global warming poses a far greater emergency than, say, terrorism. It is important to rectify this problem, so we don't leave the next generation with an unfixable mess. Progress toward combating climate change requires acts of good global citizenship and for people to make changes and sacrifices.

Storytelling Explanation. I have lived in this state all of my life, but after five hurricanes made landfall in 2020, I am thinking maybe my family should find a new place to live. Our home was flooded when Katrina hit in 2005 and our home or yard has flooded three more times since. I always thought all the talk about climate change was overblown, but after this year I am not so sure. I recently read an article in the paper that stated if the Earth continues to warm, caused largely by carbon dioxide being released from vehicles, there are likely to be even more big hurricanes in the future.

These three explanations stem from an engaging collaboration during an economics and tax research project with two of my friends.[7]

What we initially found is when talking about a contentious topic like climate change, the manner in which we appeal to people—logical, reasons, and storytelling approaches—can have varying impacts on the conversation depending on how the receiver processes or frames information. The point is there are different ways to explain the same idea depending on who you are talking with.

An especially fascinating aspect of our study revolved around participants with deeply entrenched and polarized climate beliefs, ranging from staunch positivity to vehement negativity. These individuals, who are often resistant to influence, posed a unique challenge. When we focused on this subset, our earlier findings became even more pronounced. It became evident some individuals hold beliefs so firmly they remain unyielding—a reality we found unfortunate, given the diverse perspectives and the range of willingness to compromise observed within this group.

However, amid these challenges, a glimmer of hope emerged. The majority of participants in our study demonstrated a remarkable openness to compromise, especially when tax policies were explained using various approaches. This crucial insight underscores the potent influence of explanations in nudging people toward new perspectives and behavioral change.

Deconstructing the Explanation Sandwich

How is it that some individuals effortlessly make the intricate seem straightforward? They are so good at it that it looks effortless. Malcolm Gladwell stands out as an exemplary figure in this regard. His mastery of explanation is showcased vividly in his bestselling works, including *The Tipping Point, Blink, Outliers, What the Dog Saw,* and *David and Goliath*.

Delving into Gladwell's books, it becomes evident his adeptness at explanation stems from his multifaceted experiences as a journalist, author, public speaker, and staff writer for the *New Yorker*. However, what might not be immediately apparent in Gladwell's writing is his skill in posing incisive and thought-provoking questions, which is a fundamental element in the art of explanation. In the paradigm of the "explanation sandwich," these questions serve as the essential ingredients, determining the structure and depth of the explanation.

Masterful questions, strategically formulated and deeply pondered, lay the groundwork for insightful explanations. Gladwell's ability to pose these probing queries is key to crafting his compelling narratives. His inquiries delve into the complexities of human behavior, societal trends, and the intricacies of success, setting him up to provide readers with an insightful understanding of the world around them. His questions, meticulously asked before, during, and after the writing process, elevated Gladwell's explanations to a level of unparalleled clarity and depth.

Consider some of the insightful questions Gladwell likely pondered during his exploration of diverse topics:

- How can one spark a trend that spreads like wildfire or transform a product into a coveted must-have item?
- What factors influence our instinctual decisions and why do we make the gut choices we do?
- What are the specific circumstances that pave the way for people to achieve extraordinary success in various fields?
- What is the significance of focusing on a singular goal as opposed to a diversified one, as exemplified in the ketchup conundrum (mustard comes in dozens of varieties, while ketchup has always stayed the same)?
- Why do underdogs emerge victorious in situations where the odds are overwhelmingly stacked against them?

Gladwell's meticulous exploration of these questions exemplifies the big-time impact that thoughtful inquiry can have on the explanation process. By studying his approach and adopting similar methods of questioning, we can uncover valuable insights that enhance our ability to convey complex ideas with clarity and precision. As we delve deeper into the art of explanation, we find well-crafted questions serve as the cornerstone enabling us to unravel the intricacies of the world and share our understanding with others in a compelling and engaging manner.

The second crucial element in the explanation sandwich involves the explanation and extrapolation itself. An explanation gains exceptional value when it extends beyond the immediate conversation and finds relevance in diverse scenarios. A remarkable example of this lies in the work of Steven Levitt and Stephen Dubner, authors of *Freakonomics*.[8] Their brilliance is not merely in presenting intriguing topics but in choosing subjects with broad and impactful appeal, unveiling hidden complexities in everyday situations.

In their book, Levitt and Dubner delve into seemingly unrelated topics such as cheating sumo wrestlers, drug dealers living at home with their parents, the influence of legalized abortion on crime rates, and information control around professionals like mechanics, doctors, or sales agents. Through their meticulous analysis, they reveal surprising yet profound implications for how we perceive the world. They challenge prevailing notions, debunking myths like the assumed relationship between quality parenting and educational outcomes.

What sets their work apart is not just their ability to explain these concepts clearly but also their aptitude for extrapolating the implications into a broader context. Their artistry lies in illuminating the far-reaching consequences of the concepts and patterns they're explaining. This talent is not limited to their books; it resonates in Dubner's podcasts, where he consistently demonstrates this ability across a wide array of topics. Each explanation is not an isolated event but a gateway to understanding the broader implications, adding depth and context to their insights. This application of explanation—revealing the wider significance of concepts through extrapolation—forms the critical second layer of the explanation sandwich, enhancing the impact of their work and providing a valuable lesson in effective communication and understanding.

Now to go beyond the intriguing questions and the wide-ranging impacts, let's bite into the meat of the matter—or think of it as the sizzling roasted vegetables for our non-meat enthusiasts or those who prefer a meat-free analogy. Explaining, you see, doesn't need to be a convoluted affair. And who better to school us in this fine art than a negotiator? Picture a negotiator's patience, creativity, confidence, and those razor-sharp listening skills—witnessing them at work is much like watching a delightful culinary dance.

Chris Voss stands as an exemplary figure in the realm of negotiation. His experience spans high-stakes, high-stress situations involving complex conflicts such as kidnapping, terrorism, and bank robberies in bustling metropolises. Negotiation is his forte, and he has applied his skills not only within renowned institutions like the FBI but also on international platforms such as Scotland Yard and Harvard Law School. What sets Chris apart is not just his ability to navigate these challenging scenarios, but his unique approach grounded in emotional intelligence and human connection.

Central to Chris Voss's philosophy, as outlined in his acclaimed book *Never Split the Difference*,[9] is a humble willingness to engage with individuals of all types on an emotional conversational level. His key insight is about the power of genuine connection. Chris advocates for the art of active listening and strategic questioning. By truly engaging with people and understanding their needs, emotions, and desires, negotiators can establish trust, forge bonds, and, most importantly, chart a clear path forward. It's not merely about saying yes to every demand; in fact, the strategic use of "no" is equally pivotal. By discerning and eliminating what one doesn't want, negotiators can carve out a focused and effective negotiation strategy.

Chris Voss's approach highlights the critical impact of empathy and understanding in the explanation process. By delving into the emotional landscape of the parties involved, negotiators can unearth shared interests, uncover hidden motivations, and establish common ground. This empathetic approach doesn't just build rapport; it lays the foundation for fruitful outcomes and fostering collaboration.

In essence, Chris Voss's teachings emphasize the importance of human connection in conversation. By embracing active listening, thoughtful questioning, and empathetic understanding, negotiators can transform adversarial discussions into cooperative dialogues. This approach not only enriches the negotiation experience but also enhances the likelihood of reaching agreements that satisfy all parties involved. Chris Voss's lessons serve as a guide, leading negotiators toward a more empathetic and effective approach, where emotional intelligence becomes the linchpin of successful conversations.

Chris Voss's methods encompass various strategies for assisting individuals to articulate their perspectives effectively. The challenge lies in grasping the essence of what someone is trying to convey. Chris emphasizes the importance of asking probing questions, a practice that demonstrates genuine interest in what the other person is saying and helps the speaker refine their point. Summarizing the speaker's points can also serve as a litmus test to evaluate one's understanding of their explanation. When uncertainty persists, employing well-thought-out open-ended questions, prepared in advance, can delve deeper into the speaker's thoughts. Examples include inquiries like: "What do you mean by that?" or "How do you envision this working in practice?" These approaches all converge on Chris's ultimate goal: clarifying what someone truly desires as a basis for effective communication going forward.

Better Explanations for Better Conversations

I often recall Paulo Coelho's seemingly apathetic remark: "Don't waste your time with explanations: people only hear what they want to hear." While I'm uncertain of the context in which he made this statement, my perspective on explanations has shifted significantly away from Coelho's view, especially since my time in Japan. I've become a big proponent of studying and learning about how we articulate our thoughts and ideas.

In the realm of communication, simplicity is paramount. People tend to disengage when explanations become convoluted or unclear. A close friend of mine, Pablo (not to be confused with Paulo), who is well versed in the world of research, emphasized the power of simplicity, even when crafting high-level research manuscripts tailored for a specialized scholarly audience. His advice resonated deeply with me. Whether you're penning a research paper or explaining concepts in everyday conversations, the principles remain consistent: simplicity and clarity should be your guiding stars.

Consider the explanation sandwich approach, a framework emphasizing simplicity while ensuring clarity—great questions, extended applications, engagement in the conversation within the explanation.

I offer three ways to approach your explanations: Mechanistic explanations, characterized by a step-by-step depiction of causal links (such as how A leads to B, B leads to C, and so forth), create a tight logical connection. When deploying this approach, the coherence in your reasoning simplifies the message, making it easier for your audience to grasp. Reasons-based explanations, on the other hand, rely on strong facts and compelling reasons. The more robust your evidence, the more easily you can communicate your perspective. Deploying this style enables you to fortify your viewpoint with irrefutable logic, enhancing the clarity of your message. Finally, storytelling explanations harness the power of narratives to evoke emotions. By crafting powerful and relatable stories, you can create an emotional connection with your audience, making your message memorable and impactful.

Incorporating these explanation styles into your communication repertoire equips you with a set of versatile tools. Whether you're navigating the intricacies of a research paper or engaging in everyday conversations, these techniques will enhance your ability to communicate effectively, ensuring your message resonates clearly and powerfully with your audience. So, tuck these techniques into your toolbox and use them to sharpen your skills in the art of explanation in every conversation and written endeavor.

Sharpen your communication approach to explain your position effectively.

TAKE ACTION!

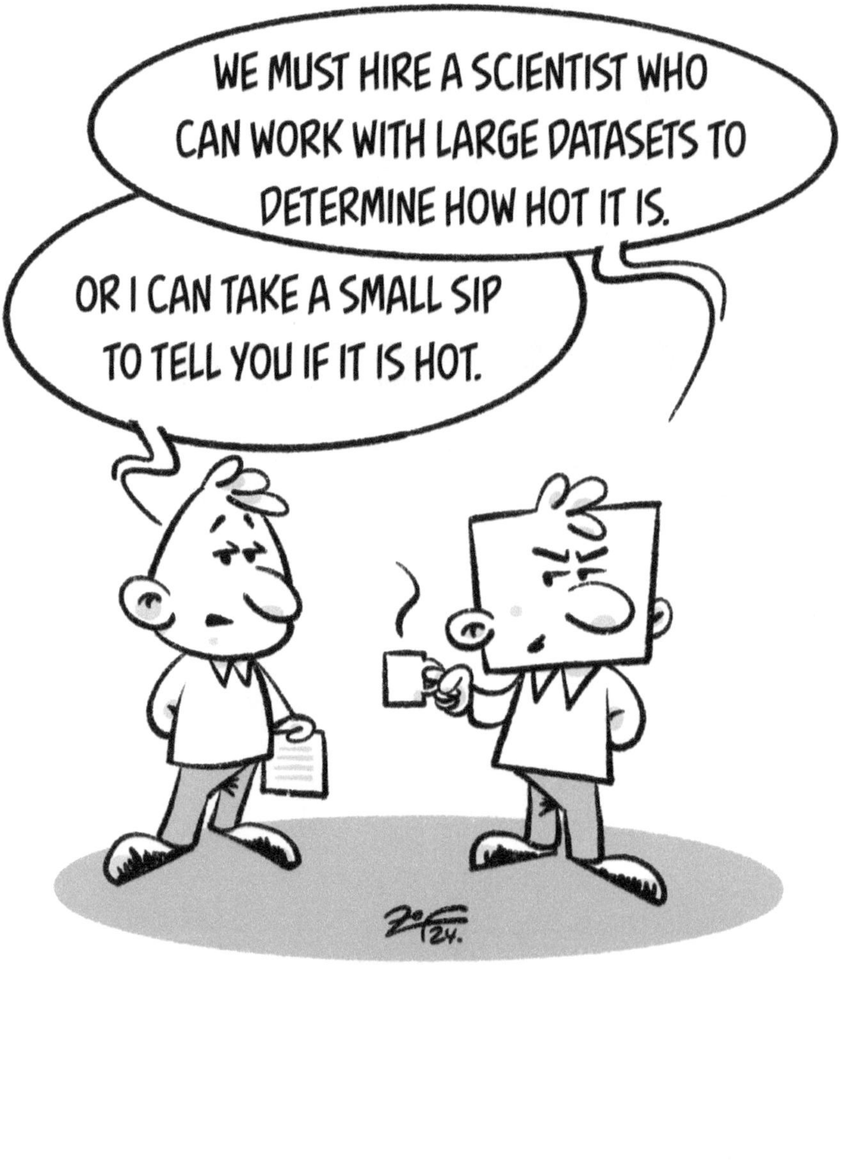
WE MUST HIRE A SCIENTIST WHO CAN WORK WITH LARGE DATASETS TO DETERMINE HOW HOT IT IS.
OR I CAN TAKE A SMALL SIP TO TELL YOU IF IT IS HOT.

Chapter Seven

Small Steps, Giant Leaps: Exploring Small-Scale Experiments

"Observation is a passive science, experimentation an active science."
—Claude Bernard

Uncorking the Joys of Wine

I've had the pleasure of immersing myself in the captivating heart of Chile, a country with a vibrant football (soccer) culture, where the melodious clinks of wine glasses sound at every meal and lively conversations often pair with the aromatic waft of barbeques. With each visit, Chile has unfailingly embraced me with open arms, unveiling its natural treasures, robust wine, and remarkable people.

One of the gems in Chile's winemaking industry that has captivated my attention is Emiliana Organic Vineyards. Stepping into this verdant sanctuary, I found myself amid one of the world's largest organic wine producers, a sprawling agricultural area of more than 800 certified organic hectares, sprawling over seven valleys in central Chile.

Emiliana's story is a tribute to the harmony between nature and craftsmanship. What initially began as a conventional wine producer in 1986 evolved into a remarkable exemplar of the journey toward organic enlightenment in 1998. Today, their commitment to organic production extends steadfastly across 100 percent of their vineyards. Embracing the ethos of organic viticulture, Emiliana champions a philosophy that resonates with nature's rhythms. Here, the grapes are nurtured without the interference of synthetic inputs, eschewing the use of pesticides and fertilizers. In their quest for sustainability, Emiliana harmoniously manages natural resources in a process that intertwines with rich biodiversity, culminating in wines echoing the very heart of Chilean terroir.

My experiences at Emiliana Organic Vineyards have been nothing short of extraordinary, unveiling a world where the art of winemaking is in lockstep with environmental stewardship. Each glass of their meticulously crafted wine is a sip of Chile's soul, a testament to the synergy between the land, the vine, and the dedicated hands that craft these liquid masterpieces. In this haven of organic viticulture, I have not only savored outstanding wines but also witnessed a tremendous respect for the Earth, inspiring me to delve deeper into the realm of Chilean viniculture.

Engaging in a partnership with Emiliana for a research endeavor might appear to some as an indulgence, but to me, it was an intriguing fusion of close friendship, empirical data collection, and the artistry of winemaking. My friends Pablo and Kenneth and I initiated our collaboration with Emiliana, sparking my curiosity about the connection between research and wine—a pairing that proved to be unexpectedly harmonious.

During my time delving into the world of Emiliana, what struck me most was their passionate embracing of biodynamic practices. Their approach, encompassing unique Demeter methods[1] like cosmic force acknowledgment, the visualization of soil as a living entity, and reducing reliance on external inputs, demonstrated their holistic view of winemaking. In this intricate approach, the farmer and winemaker intertwined with both the visible and invisible forces of nature, fostering the creation of thriving ecosystems.[2] The team's genuine commitment to their environment was palpable. Their closeness to nature was more than a mere sentiment—it was a way of being.

Yet beyond the technicalities, what stuck with me was Emiliana's ethos of experimentation. They displayed a remarkable willingness to observe and explore novel approaches to winemaking, a testament to their dedication to sustainability and innovation. Witnessing this ethos firsthand, I learned that embracing experimentation is not just a methodology; it's a mindset—a way of fostering harmony between human ingenuity and the natural world. Emiliana's approach left a lasting impression, teaching me the invaluable lesson that in the realm of winemaking, and beyond, embracing change and exploration can yield remarkable outcomes.

One way in which Emiliana pairs experimentation and ecological stewardship is by exploring the intricate dynamics of living systems, vividly manifested in the estate's reconstruction of predator–prey relationships. In their quest to minimize chemical usage and synthetic preparations, Emiliana keenly observes and comprehends the natural predators inhabiting the estate. A notable instance of this approach involved the introduction of chickens, a natural and ingenious solution to combat pests such as white worms. Through this innovative experiment, the delicate balance of nature is subtly orchestrated, where former predators become prey, setting off a chain reaction of new animal relationships. This harmonious interplay not only curtails pest populations without using synthetic pesticides but also enriches the overall ecological vitality of the estate, showcasing Emiliana's commitment to fostering a sustainable and thriving ecosystem through experimentation.

Experimentation at Emiliana involves the vital process of sensemaking, a reflective practice. Over time, they have discerned that soil fertility hinges on perceiving the soil as a living entity, recognizing the intricate interactions among its inhabitants. Vines, integral to this living web, coexist with bacteria, fungi, worms, and beetles in a symphony of symbiosis, each organism contributing to the others' well-being.

For Emiliana, experimentation is an art rooted in consensus building and observing biodiversity outcomes. Their approach has introduced innovative practices that enhance the vineyard's overall health, unveiling interconnected living processes and elevating the quality of the wines they produce.

David Blaine said it well: "Whether you're shuffling a deck of cards or holding your breath, magic is pretty simple: it comes down to training, practice, and experimentation, followed up by ridiculous pursuit and relentless perseverance."[3] The common motivational rhetoric often urges us to "take action today," but without forethought and guidance, that can be daunting. Only, after thoughtful contemplation and discussions, the transition to action becomes accessible. And experimentation provides a tangible and meaningful entry point for action. Mini-experiments can help us to test new routes and appreciate other ways of being and doing, thus reducing narrow-blinded thinking and contempt toward alternative views.

Figure 7.1

Talk
about it
Think
Take action
1. Experiment

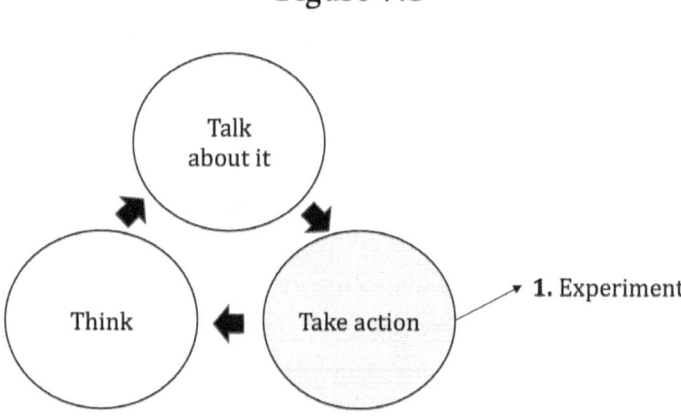

Combating narrow-blinded thinking requires experimentation.

Winner, Winner, Chicken Dinner

John Lasseter has a good quote: "With science, there is this culture of experimentation, and most of the time, those experiments fail."[4] On the face of it, this can sound a bit depressing, because navigating the path to action can be overwhelming, especially when confronted with a daunting sense of time ("It's so far into the future!") and magnitude ("It's too big of a challenge!").

Karl Weick, a renowned psychologist from the University of Michigan, probed deep into this area of (in)action, unveiling an insightful concept known as the theory of small wins. According to Weick, a "small win" refers to a tangible, complete, and implemented outcome of moderate importance—an achievable task, essentially, a manageable chunk of work.[5] It might seem trivial at first glance; making your bed, taking a short walk, or completing a minor task may not appear monumental. Yet, these seemingly insignificant victories, when accumulated throughout a day, a week, or a lifetime, amount to a myriad of accomplishments.

The brilliance of Weick's theory lies in its ability to confront a significant roadblock: cognitive overload. The sheer volume of information associated with decision-making, understanding complex situations, or taking big steps toward action often overwhelms us and leads to paralysis. Weick contends that framing tasks as small wins provides an effective solution to this challenge. Complex systems, ranging from the vast Library of Congress to intricate industrial facilities like a DuPont factory, the Environmental Protection Agency (EPA), or even NASA, employ the concept of small wins to achieve their monumental missions. While individuals vary in their capacity to handle information, the concept of small wins remains universally applicable.

When confronted with overwhelming information, many individuals experience an analysis meltdown, rendering them powerless in the face of massive global problems. The sheer scale and complexity of these issues often lead to depersonalization, making it difficult for people to feel a sense of agency. Embracing the theory of small wins offers a powerful antidote to this sense of helplessness and the fallout from narrow-blinded thinking. By breaking down colossal challenges into manageable tasks, individuals can bypass the debilitating effects of information overload and move toward action.

Each small win serves as a stepping stone, empowering individuals to move beyond analysis paralysis and take meaningful action. As these victories accumulate, they not only bolster confidence but also demonstrate the potential for transformative change. Whether it's tidying up your immediate surroundings or initiating a small act of kindness, the ripple effects of these seemingly minor triumphs can contribute to significant shifts in personal and societal contexts. In essence, the theory of small wins charts a walkable path toward impactful change in a world often plagued by complexity and enormity.

Teresa Amabile and Steve Kramer's research on small wins provides valuable insights into our daily lives and overall well-being.[6] Contrary to the common belief that significant victories, such as winning the lottery, guarantee lasting happiness, Amabile and Kramer discovered it's the small, frequent wins, like going outside or practicing yoga daily, which have a profound and enduring impact on our happiness.

Reflecting on the past few days, have you perhaps overlooked some of these small wins in your own life? Whether it was completing a workout, making a meaningful connection, or achieving a benchmark in a personal goal, these seemingly minor accomplishments deserve recognition. So congratulations! It's important to acknowledge the significance of these often-overlooked victories. Embracing and celebrating these small wins not only enhances your overall sense of happiness but also reinforces the idea that meaningful, lasting contentment often stems from the accumulation of everyday moments of triumph.

The Promise of Microfinance Experiments

Esther Duflo and Abhijit Banerjee, distinguished economists from the Massachusetts Institute of Technology, have made significant contributions to the field of development economics. Notably, this dynamic duo has been honored with the Nobel Prize in Economics for their exceptional work. At MIT, Duflo and Banerjee operate a vast laboratory dedicated to dissecting significant issues like poverty, breaking them down into manageable components and posing smaller, more specific questions that demand rigorous answers. Over the span of two decades, they have extensively researched and published numerous articles in the realm of randomized control trials, focusing on poverty alleviation strategies.

At the heart of their research lies the innovative method of randomized control trials (RCTs), a powerful tool for assessing the effectiveness of interventions. This methodological approach involves meticulous planning: First, participants are carefully evaluated for eligibility, ensuring they meet the study's specific criteria. Subsequently, they are randomly assigned to different groups, with one group receiving the intervention—such as specialized business training—while the other serves as a control group. After a designated period, a comprehensive follow-up ensues, during which data is collected and meticulously analyzed to ascertain the impact of the intervention.

Duflo and Banerjee's pioneering work not only illuminates the complexities of poverty alleviation but also underscores the significance of experiments. Through their relentless dedication, they have significantly advanced our understanding of effective interventions, offering valuable insights that continue to shape the field of development economics.

Experiments, such as RCTs, are intriguing because what might initially appear as a brilliant intervention idea might not yield the expected results when put into practice. An illustrative example of this phenomenon was discussed in a June 2020 article in *Finance & Development*, which highlighted a specific case of failure:

One that famously flopped was to replace open-fire cooking used by 3 billion of the world's poorest people with more efficient, less polluting stoves under the Global Alliance for Clean Cookstoves initiative. The $400 million project was backed by the United Nations and launched by former US Secretary of State Hillary Clinton in 2010. It set out to reduce indoor air pollution, which kills 2 million people a year, while empowering women and helping the environment. After initial success, millions of stoves built in India were largely abandoned after four years.[7]

The stove intervention may be labeled a failure, but is it really? Many scholars behind experiments view failures as crucial components of their extensive research efforts. Even when an intervention yields a negative result—when it doesn't work as anticipated—it provides invaluable insights. Each "no" from these experiments contributes essential knowledge. By accumulating these successes and failures, researchers gain a deeper understanding of the complex landscape they're exploring. It's akin to assembling pieces of a puzzle; every "yes" and "no" adds information about how the fragments fit together, gradually forming a clearer picture of the challenges at hand.

This evolution of experiments yields valuable insights for poverty researchers and governments alike. It offers an opportunity to delve into cultural and geographic nuances, providing gradually deeper understanding of diverse communities. These experiments illuminate pathways to build regional capacity effectively, demonstrating not only what works but also what doesn't, thus enabling policymakers to make informed decisions.

Moreover, these experiments play a pivotal role in uplifting communities and enhancing resilience. By understanding what interventions succeed and where they fall short, communities can learn how to better support one another. This collective knowledge becomes a powerful tool, enabling societies to build robust networks, strengthen community bonds, and foster resilience in the face of challenges. In essence, these experiments, whether they yield positive or negative outcomes, contribute to a continuous process of learning, shaping the future of poverty alleviation efforts and community development.

Experimentation in Uganda

Extreme poverty stands as a formidable and intricate challenge, casting a shadow over the lives of millions. In Sub-Saharan Africa, nearly half of the 910 million residents live on less than USD $1.25 per day—a stark definition of extreme poverty.[8] This harsh reality deprives families of fundamental necessities like food, education, and healthcare for their children, perpetuating poverty's vicious cycle. However, amid these daunting circumstances, a glimmer of hope emerges from the collective efforts of dedicated researchers and organizations. They firmly believe finance holds the key to a viable solution, sparking a growing movement that aims to break the chains of poverty and usher in a brighter future for those in need.

After talking with executives at microfinance lending organizations, I came to realize that across different regions of the world, loan repayment was an issue, as were the high interest rates charged. And at the core, there were still questions of whether these loans improved the wellness of the families receiving them. I became most interested in how both the recipient of a microfinance loan and the lending organization could balance aid with institutional sustainability.

So, what did I do? I ran my own experiment![9] I embarked on a project aimed at tackling a crucial challenge faced by microfinance institutions: how to provide developmental programs while maintaining financial stability. The sustainability of lending organizations is vital, as it determines their ability to offer long-term opportunities to individuals in need. Lending to people in developing nations is inherently risky for both the lender and the borrower, making it essential to find innovative solutions.

After several immersive experiences in Uganda to gain a deeper understanding of the country and its people, I conducted a randomized control trial. The focus was on supporting women entrepreneurs in rural Uganda by helping them to start their own businesses. Women were divided into three groups: one group received financial assistance alone, another received financial assistance coupled with well-being mentorship, and the third group received financial assistance, business training, and well-being mentorship.

The unique aspect of the experiment was the inclusion of well-being mentorship sessions, known as "sensitizations," conducted during loan collection meetings. These one-to-two-hour sessions took place at the homes of group members on a rotating monthly basis. Facilitated by a respected *senga* (paternal aunt), the mentorship covered crucial topics such as HIV/AIDS testing and counseling, family dynamics, the importance of children's education, community development, home sanitation, and food/water security. As part of this mentorship, borrowers were educated on safe water procedures, sanitation, hygiene, and waste management. Each borrower was required to have a latrine, drying rack, and tippy tap (a handwashing device), and was tested for HIV/AIDS.

The multifaceted approach aimed not only to empower women entrepreneurs financially but also to enhance their overall well-being and community impact. Through this experiment, I sought to answer questions about models that could address the multifaceted challenges faced by borrowers in developing nations, paving the way for a more inclusive and supportive future.

A significant revelation arising from this experiment pertained to the actual long-term impact of providing business training. It became evident that incorporating business training into the loan conditions might not be the most effective approach. Defining what constitutes effective training proved challenging, and the financial viability of this approach from the organizational perspective raised serious concerns. Business training, as it turns out, comes at a hefty cost. I found that rather than expending resources on trainers, redirecting these funds toward supporting more entrepreneurs might be a more strategic allocation. Surprisingly, little attention has been devoted to assessing the long-term cost-benefit ratio of such training, a crucial aspect to maximize benefits for both borrowers and lenders. So this was an interesting finding from a small experiment, and it demonstrates that in the realm of microfinance, a meticulous reevaluation of the role and effectiveness of business training is warranted.

In stark contrast, the results underscored the value and affordability of well-being mentoring. In my research paper, I emphasized this component might offer the best "bang for the buck," aligning the interests of both women entrepreneurs and microfinance lending institutions. The evidence pointed toward the invaluable impact of well-being mentoring, shedding light on a cost-effective and meaningful way to support borrowers. The revelation highlights the need for a shift in focus, urging a closer examination of the potential dividends of investing in the holistic well-being of borrowers, ultimately ensuring a more impactful and sustainable microfinance model.

Rapid Prototyping in Life

In the 1980s, the concept of rapid prototyping emerged in the manufacturing realm, revolutionizing how models and parts were created. The process involved fabricating scaled parts using computer-aided design, enabling companies to produce trial components for testing new applications or methods. The objective was to explore innovative ways of production, assess associated costs, evaluate product fit, and road-test product durability.

Rapid prototyping seamlessly aligns with the theory of small wins and running mini-experiments in our own lives. While rapid prototyping has its origins in sophisticated manufacturing and technology industries, its application extends to our lives as a beneficial method of taking gradual action. Just as in the manufacturing world, rapid prototyping in our lives offers the advantages of lower costs and innovative decision-making approaches.

These small, action-oriented experiments help us to test out new logics and alternative views, keeping us from being stuck in old ways of narrow-blinded thinking and contempt.

Exemplar Small Wins

It is essential to underscore the significance of celebrating small victories found through experimentation. Breaking down monumental tasks into manageable chunks not only simplifies the process but also ensures tangible and sustainable advancement. Having supportive allies or mentors can further enhance this process, offering valuable guidance while helping you steer clear of potential obstacles.

There are many examples throughout history of individuals who achieved great actions and contributions by having a small experiment orientation across a variety of fields. These individuals are akin to a hydra—complex, adaptive, and versatile. Take Pablo Picasso, the renowned Spanish artist, for instance. His experimentation knew no bounds, and he epitomized persistence as he ventured into various media, excelling as a sculptor, painter, designer, and playwright. Similarly, Leonardo Da Vinci, renowned for masterpieces like the *Mona Lisa* and *The Last Supper*, experimented across diverse disciplines including engineering, architecture, and astronomy, earning recognition as a polymath experimenter. Leonardo's visionary sketches, including designs for bicycles and helicopters, showcase his unbridled curiosity and experimental spirit.

In the realm of innovation, the Turkish experimenter Ismail Al-Jazari stands out. His remarkable gift lay not just in his inventions but also in his ability to document and share his ideas with others. His seminal work *The Book of Knowledge of Ingenious Mechanical Devices*[10] meticulously outlines the design, manufacturing, and assembly of his ingenious machines, ranging from alarm clocks to washing devices and robots. Al-Jazari's legacy endures, not only for his creations but also for his ability to articulate and disseminate the knowledge he amassed through experimentation.

In essence, these historical examples underscore the diverse facets of experimenters—visionaries who not only explore uncharted territories but also share their discoveries, enriching the collective knowledge of society. There is not just one way to experiment, but there are commonalities shared among various methods. All require a deep curiosity, collaboration with allies, and a willingness to boldly navigate the intricate landscape of discovery and progress in the face of failure. In the exhilarating world of experimenters, every challenge is an opportunity, every setback a stepping stone, and every experiment a thrilling adventure into the unknown.

Experimenters have the ability to imagine alternatives. Take the awe-inspiring journey of J.K. Rowling, the literary sorceress who enchanted over 500 million readers with her spellbinding tales of a young wizard named Harry Potter. With boundless passion and unmatched creativity, Rowling brought Hogwarts and its magical inhabitants to life, leaving an indelible mark on the world—an extraordinary testament to the experimenter DNA.

Or, how about Lee Byung-Chul, the pioneering visionary behind Samsung? This bold business experimenter dared to dream big and, more importantly, took courageous small leaps into uncharted territories. His daring experiments led to a dazzling array of innovations: phones connecting us, helicopter engines soaring the skies, cars reimagining travel, toilet seats redefining comfort, TVs bringing stories to life, vacuums automatically tidying our homes, and medical devices saving lives. Each creation is a tribute to his audacious spirit, demonstrating that experimenters don't just imagine alternatives—they bring them to life through action!

And who could forget the remarkable journey of Mahatma Gandhi, the quintessential adventurer whose life was an array of brave experiments? Gandhi's indomitable spirit and unwavering commitment to truth transformed not only his life but also the fate of a nation. His exploration of new approaches and alternative perspectives resonates through the pages of his autobiography. From childhood experiments with fundamental choices to his experiences with ethnic tensions, wars, and the relentless struggle against British colonial rule, every chapter in his life was an experiment—evidence to the power of relentless determination and the pursuit of truth.

 Small wins through experimentation move the wheels of action.

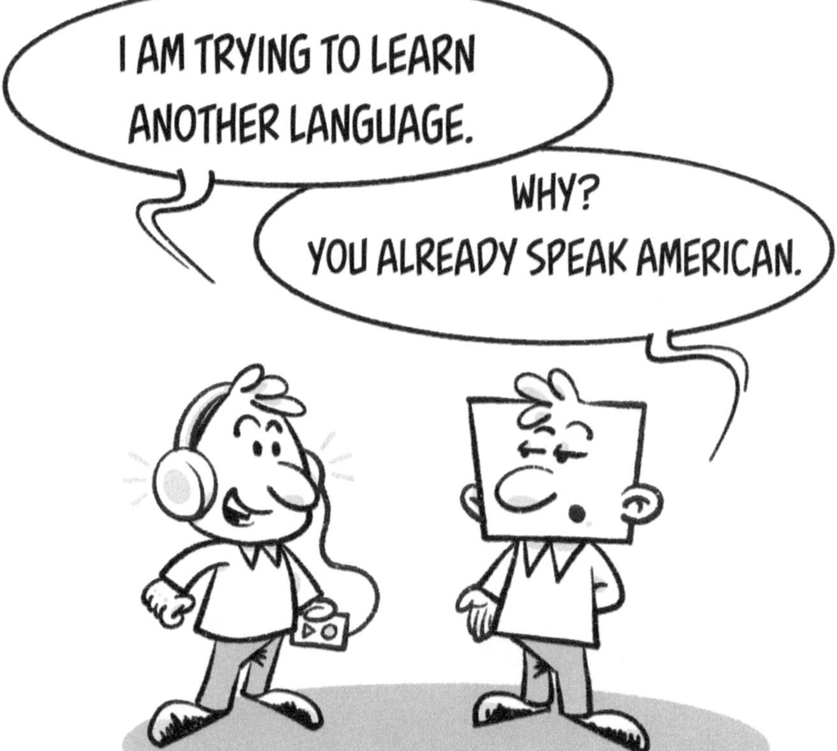
I AM TRYING TO LEARN ANOTHER LANGUAGE.
WHY? YOU ALREADY SPEAK AMERICAN.

Chapter Eight

Improvement Doesn't Happen by Chance

"Inaction breeds doubt and fear. Action breeds confidence and courage. If you want to conquer fear, don't sit home and think about it. Go out and get busy."
—Dale Carnegie

Navigating the Journey of Learning

As I write this book, I find myself in my tenth year residing in America. During this time, I have encountered various reactions from friends and family in Canada, Ireland, and England, who often wonder, "Why would you want to live in that country?" To their inquiries, I have offered my clarifications, honed and refined, over the years.

Initially, the decision to move to the United States was simply the start of another chapter in our global adventure. My wife and I, accompanied by our faithful canine companions, are seasoned nomads, accustomed to a life of constant movement and exploration. Our free-wandering lifestyle is largely feasible due to my profession as a professor. Being in academia has afforded me the flexibility to traverse the globe.

Our journey stateside started with an intriguing opportunity in Montana, where a university was in search of an accounting and/or tax professor. Serendipity smiled upon me as the hiring committee saw me as a good candidate to fill the position. And so, our family found itself embracing yet another new beginning, captivated by the prospect of new knowledge and experiences in this beautifully complex country.

Despite the initial skepticism we encountered from acquaintances abroad, our time in America has been marked by enriching experiences, deep social connections, and extraordinary learning opportunities. In Montana, our lives were positioned at 5,000 feet above sea level, amid majestic mountains that painted a breathtaking panorama around us. The rugged terrain not only served as a scenic backdrop but also as an invitation to adventure, offering some of the finest skiing, most exhilarating mountain biking, and best idyllic camping in the entire country. It was in this blue-sky environment that we found kindred spirits—remarkable individuals who shared our passion for the great outdoors. Forming bonds with these extraordinary people was nothing short of a stroke of good fortune.

Now on the East Coast, I am reflecting more on my journey and contemplating the question of why I take pride in calling this country home. I am compelled to acknowledge the multifaceted aspects that are the United States of America. While some may perceive the sheer size of its population—a staggering 332 million or so individuals—merely as a capitalist statistic, I view it through a different lens. This nation stands as a testament to the resilience, intellect, innovation, and entrepreneurial spirit of its people.

Beyond the numerical magnitude, America boasts a wealth of education, nurturing brilliant minds that lead the way in various fields of study. It is a hub of innovation, where groundbreaking ideas flourish and entrepreneurial ventures thrive. The United States is not merely a landmass; it is a diverse mosaic of cultures, landscapes, and culinary traditions. From the sandy shores of California to the lush forests

Chapter Eight: Improvement Doesn't Happen by Chance

of Vermont, each state paints its unique stroke on the canvas of this vast nation. In essence, America embodies a collection of fifty distinct countries, each with its own character and charm.

One of the most remarkable sides of this nation is its generosity, ranking consistently high on the global scale of philanthropy and humanitarian efforts. The spirit of giving back is deeply ingrained in the American ethos, fostering a sense of community and solidarity. Upon close inspection, what may have initially appeared to me as "over-the-top Americanism" has, over the course of more than a decade, revealed itself to be a genuine sense of pride.

Yes, critics might accuse me of naivety, but I choose to embrace the beauty I see in this land, in its people, and in the vibrant blend of cultures that largely coexist within its borders. America, with all its challenges and complexities, remains a magnificent place to live—a land teeming with extraordinary individuals, diverse traditions, and an unwavering spirit of resilience. It is a tribute to the enduring allure of this place I affectionately call the United States of America.

During my time in the US, I've gleaned an important lesson that has reverberated deeply within me: a grit mentality. Embarking on the journey of acquiring new skills or knowledge can dramatically alter one's perspective, opening doors to experiences previously unimagined. This revelation became strikingly evident to me in the rugged landscapes of Montana, where I found myself immersed in a series of endeavors that reshaped my understanding of the urge to expand my horizons.

One significant chapter of my learning odyssey unfolded in the wild expanses of Montana, where I embraced the art of hunting. Despite my unfamiliarity with firearms, I took the daunting step of picking up a rifle, a decision that initially filled me with trepidation. The weight of the weapon in my hands, the loud reports echoing in the wilderness, and the recoil jolting through my shoulder were all intimidating. However, guided by friends who valued the ethical and conservationist aspects of hunting, I delved into this primal pursuit. Through the process, I discovered not only the gratification of sourcing my own food but also a weighty respect for nature and the sustenance it provides. Each meal on my plate became evidence of that newfound understanding; a result of my own hard work and efforts to understand the intricate balance of ecosystems.

Montana also introduced me to the world of CrossFit, a fitness regimen that melds high-intensity interval training, gymnastics, and Olympic weightlifting. Encouraged by one of my graduate students, I embraced this challenge, stepping into the gym with a mix of excitement and uncertainty. Little did I know this decision would usher in some of the healthiest and most invigorating years of my life. The supportive community I found in the CrossFit arena became a source of inspiration, teaching me not only physical endurance but also mental resilience and camaraderie.

One of the most memorable and rewarding experiences of my time in Montana was stepping into the arena of automotive restoration. Two local experts, who were incredibly generous with their knowledge and time, joined me in the ambitious project of reviving a 1938 International truck, a cherished relic from my wife's grandfather's farm in Canada. Though the truck arrived as a heartfelt birthday gift, it clearly needed extensive work—lacking power steering, shocks, brakes, and more. Undeterred by the daunting challenge, I embraced the opportunity to learn from scratch. With the expert team offering me much patient guidance, together we breathed new life into the old vehicle. From reviving the engine and overhauling the transmission to installing a new steering system and crafting a sturdy wood bed for the truck, I found immeasurable joy in the process of hands-on learning. The truck became a tangible verification of my newfound interest in craft and the fusion of tradition and modernity.

Through these diverse experiences, I've come to cherish the boundless potential that lies within the act of learning. Each new skill acquired not only broadens my horizons but also enriches my life with a deeper appreciation for the world and its infinite possibilities. Montana, with its scenic beauty and warm-hearted inhabitants, was the perfect incubator for these transformative lessons, reminding me the pursuit of knowledge is a journey worth undertaking.

Ah, the wisdom of Yoda again—a pint-sized sage with an affinity for unconventional life advice. "Do or do not, there is no try," he quipped, cutting through any equivocation like a lightsaber through butter.[1] It's not just about giving it a go; it's about diving headfirst into the cold plunge pool of possibilities with a growth mindset. Mahatma Gandhi said it well, "Live as if you were to die tomorrow but learn as if you were to live forever." Learning and growth are antidotes to the narrow-blinded thinking that too often clouds our judgment.

Figure 8.1

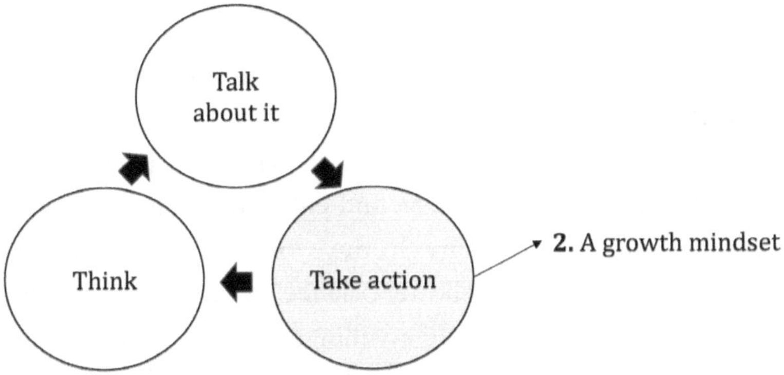

Combating narrow-blinded thinking requires a growth mindset.

Cultivating Courage, Embracing Growth

As we delve into the realms of fear, growth, and action, we find an insightful guide in the works of Dr. Carol Dweck, a distinguished psychologist and professor of psychology at the illustrious Stanford University. With a wealth of expertise in the fields of personality and development, Dr. Dweck has dedicated years to unraveling the intricate layers of human motivation, personality dynamics, and social and personal development. Her extensive research illuminates the mental pathways that lead to personal growth and transformation, sparking intriguing debates within the psychological community.

At the heart of Dr. Dweck's work lies the compelling concept of the growth mindset, a notion that has stirred both fascination and controversy. The debate revolves around differing beliefs regarding intelligence and success. On one end of the spectrum, there are proponents of the fixed mindset, asserting that intelligence is static and predetermined. On the opposing side, champions of the growth mindset argue that success is a product of unwavering determination, continuous learning, and diligent training. The tension between these perspectives has sparked debates and contemplation, challenging our understanding of human potential.

As for my own stance on the matter, I find myself navigating the nuanced middle ground of this continuum. Is hard work a catalyst for success? Undoubtedly, yes. The sweat, toil, and persistent effort we invest often yields meaningful outcomes. But are we as humans sometimes limited? Probably also, yes. Nonetheless, the idea of expanding one's horizons, embracing change, and cultivating a growth-oriented mindset holds undeniable allure. In the evolving landscape of human capability, there exists a delicate balance, where the interplay of inherent talents, hard work, and a willingness to venture beyond our comfort zones can unlock unparalleled opportunities for personal and professional growth.

Dr. Dweck's research not only challenges our beliefs about where success comes from, but also invites us to reflect on our own mindset, encouraging us to explore the connections between friction, action, and growth. In the endless realm of possibilities, where fear builds resilience and action paves the way for transformation, Dr. Dweck's insights serve as an encouraging call, guiding us toward a deeper, more generous understanding of our own potential.

Chapter Eight: Improvement Doesn't Happen by Chance

Dweck defined her view of the growth mindset in one interview:

> In a fixed mindset students believe their basic abilities, their intelligence, their talents, are just fixed traits. They have a certain amount and that's that, and then their goal becomes to look smart all the time and never look dumb. In a growth mindset students understand that their talents and abilities can be developed through effort, good teaching, and persistence. They don't necessarily think everyone's the same or anyone can be Einstein, but they believe everyone can get smarter if they work at it.[2]

In 2019, Dr. David Yeager, a researcher at The University of Texas at Austin, conducted a growth mindset experiment with a group of high school freshmen. The experiment involved the use of twenty-five-minute online modules aimed to elucidate the distinctions between a fixed mindset and a growth mindset. The results of this study were quite noteworthy, as they demonstrated the transformative potential of these educational modules.[3]

The study's findings indicated that the online modules designed to help students understand and adopt a growth mindset had a positive impact on their academic performance and educational choices. Specifically, the students who engaged with these modules showed significant improvements in their grades and were more likely to enroll in advanced math courses. This outcome underscores the influence of mindset education on shaping students' beliefs about their own abilities and, subsequently, their academic choices, achievements, and aspirations.

While there are critics who question the validity of Dweck's mindset theory due to challenges in replicating her research, there's a valuable nugget of wisdom we can still embrace in the meantime. Regardless of the ongoing debate, the act of expanding our learning through action remains undeniably positive. Cultivating a mindset centered on the desire to learn, the belief in one's ability to learn, and the priority of continuous learning is undeniably healthy. Regardless of the conclusive answer on the growth mindset theory, the proactive pursuit of knowledge and the belief in our capacity to learn stand as enduring principles for personal and intellectual growth.

In my personal pursuit of enhancing my brain's plasticity, I've embarked on an annual ritual of exploration. Each year, I eagerly dive into the depths of learning, categorizing my pursuits into three exciting realms: the tactile world of hands-on skills, the intellectually stimulating realm of academic knowledge, and the adrenaline-fueled universe of athletic endeavors. Channeling my inner artisan, I've taken up residence as a student at a woodworking school, immersing myself in the intricacies of crafting fine furniture with passion and precision. On the academic front, I challenge my mind to pursue innovative research projects, each one designed to stretch the boundaries of my intellectual horizons. The thrill of discovery propels me forward, igniting my curiosity and fueling my academic ambitions. And then there's the realm of athleticism, where I've recently embraced the wild allure of fat-tire biking. Picture me conquering snow-covered trails and sandy beaches alike, my trusty fat bike beneath me—it's hilarious and fun, come rain, snow, or sunshine.

Nothing to It but to Do It!

A growth mindset means you think it can be done and you take action to get it done. Oddly, I find inspiration in watching Ronnie Coleman's weightlifting videos, where he effortlessly lifts staggering amounts of weight, such as an impressive 800 pounds on the squat, all while exclaiming motivating phrases like "Yeah buddy!" "Light weight, baby!" and "Ain't nothin' but a peanut!" Even for non-weightlifters, his unwavering self-motivation, boundless positive energy, and unshakable belief in his abilities are truly admirable, making his YouTube videos a must-watch.

Chapter Eight: Improvement Doesn't Happen by Chance

For those unfamiliar with Ronnie Coleman, he is the winner of Mr. Olympia, the pinnacle of bodybuilding competitions—eight times over. While I am not an avid follower of bodybuilding events, I deeply respect Coleman's incredible journey from poverty to success. His story is a demonstration of resilience and unwavering commitment to personal growth, both physical and mental. What adds to his remarkable story is the fact that outside of competitive weightlifting, he pursued a career as an accountant and even served as a police officer, highlighting his dedication to community service.

Beyond the weights and accolades, Ronnie Coleman's life journey serves as an example of determination and triumph, reminding us of the boundless potential within us all. His example encourages us to push our limits, pursue our passions, and never underestimate the power of resilience and hard work, no matter the challenges we face.

If lifting weights Ronnie Coleman–style isn't quite your cup of tea, fear not, for there are many inspiring figures out there whose insatiable curiosity and relentless pursuit of knowledge serve as models for embracing the growth mindset. Consider Neil deGrasse Tyson, the eminent American astrophysicist, author, and science communicator, whose fascination with the cosmos has captivated audiences worldwide. How about Benjamin Franklin, the polymath whose intellectual appetite knew no bounds; he fed his inquisitive mind as a writer, scientist, inventor, diplomat, painter, philosopher, and publisher, leaving an indelible mark on history. There's also Elon Musk, the audacious entrepreneur who fearlessly dives into unfamiliar territories, teaching himself the intricacies of various disciplines to succeed as the founder of multiple groundbreaking organizations. Musk's ventures stand as testament to the power of self-belief and an unyielding drive for learning.

And let's not forget Aristotle, the ancient Greek whose intellectual curiosity surpasses easy description. His explorations spanned a staggering array of subjects including physics, biology, zoology, metaphysics, logic, ethics, aesthetics, poetry, drama, music, rhetoric, psychology, linguistics, economics, politics, meteorology, geology, and government. Aristotle's insatiable thirst for understanding illuminated countless fields of knowledge and laid the foundation for Western philosophy.

What unites these remarkable individuals is not just their exceptional talents, but their shared love for learning and the unwavering belief in their capacity to grow. Their stories serve as a reminder that the pursuit of knowledge isn't confined to the classroom; it's a lifelong journey fueled by curiosity, passion, and the conviction that every mind has the potential to expand and evolve.

Not too long ago, I stumbled upon a captivating research newsletter from the University of Pennsylvania that delved into the profound connection between the love of learning and happiness.[4] In this instructive piece, the author defined "love of learning" as a deep-rooted motivation to acquire new skills or knowledge, to refine existing abilities, and to persist even in the face of occasional frustrations or setbacks. The author pointed out that individuals who harbor this genuine passion for learning exhibit remarkable traits—they possess the ability to self-regulate, persevere in the face of challenges, experience a sense of autonomy, and feel profoundly resourceful.

However, what truly resonated with me was the revelation that those who harbor a love for learning also possess an unwavering belief in the realm of the possible. It's a deep emotion, one that not only fuels their curiosity but also instills in them a sense of agency over the outcomes in their lives. This potent combination of boundless curiosity and a belief in endless possibilities has far-reaching positive consequences, shaping the way they navigate challenges, embrace opportunities, and ultimately find happiness and fulfillment in their journey of continuous growth and learning.

What's the key takeaway from all this? Individuals who possess a genuine love for learning, along with a firm belief in possibility and the concept of a growth mindset, exhibit strikingly similar traits.[5] They immerse themselves in books, seeing reading as a gateway to new worlds and greater understanding. These perpetual learners are not just occasional enthusiasts; they are lifelong devotees to the pursuit of knowledge. Embracing the growth mindset, they actively seek opportunities to expand their horizons, nurturing their minds and bodies alike. They prioritize their health, indulge in diverse passions, and warmly welcome change as a catalyst for personal and intellectual evolution.

This approach to growth is grounded in the fundamental, firmly held belief that it's never too late to acquire new skills or knowledge. Those with this mindset have a contagious attitude toward self-improvement, inspiring others around them to embrace the transformative power of learning. To them, learning is synonymous with stepping out of their comfort zone, a courageous journey into the unknown. These individuals harbor no fear of failure; instead, they view setbacks as invaluable learning experiences. Unafraid to ask questions, their inquiries fuel their curiosity and perpetuate a cycle of continuous learning and personal development.

Inquisitive?

In reflecting upon my journey, two recent instances come to mind for how they vividly demonstrate the remarkable opportunities curiosity can unveil, leading to unparalleled personal and professional growth. The first unfolded in a business school where I was previously employed. Our accounting department faced a significant challenge: the imminent retirement of our singular tax professor would leave a void in both our undergraduate and graduate accounting programs. It was akin to having a sports team with a small bench—there was a critical gap that needed urgent attention. During a faculty meeting, the dean of the business school sought solutions. Seizing the moment, I volunteered to return to graduate school and earn a degree in taxation, a commitment that would span two years. My proposition was simple: if the business school funded my tuition, I would equip myself with the necessary expertise to fill the tax void in our faculty.

Little did I realize then how much this decision would impact my life. Not only did I find immense satisfaction looking into the intricacies of taxation, but it also opened doors to unexpected opportunities. One of these opportunities emerged through my involvement in the Volunteer Income Tax Program (VITA), an initiative by the Internal Revenue Service to provide free tax preparation services and invaluable assistance to low- to moderate-income individuals, persons with disabilities, the elderly, and limited English speakers. The experience of collaborating with my students to successfully run the VITA program was not only professionally rewarding but also deeply fulfilling on a personal level.

Moreover, pursuing a graduate degree in taxation inadvertently led me to attend academic tax conferences—a prospect that might not initially captivate everyone's interest, but it definitely did mine. My fortune lay in the incredible individuals I met at these conferences—some of the brightest and kindest people you could imagine. Engaging with these scholars ignited my passion for research, inspiring collaborations I never anticipated. Today, I find myself working alongside these esteemed tax researchers and contributing to the academic tax discourse. What started as a professional endeavor transformed into meaningful personal connections, as some of these researchers have become cherished friends, enriching my life in unexpected ways.

This whole course of experience highlights the transformative power of curiosity, demonstrating that the pursuit of knowledge, coupled with a willingness to explore uncharted territories, can lead to extraordinary outcomes. Embracing curiosity and asking questions have not only enriched my professional life but have also cultivated deep personal fulfillment, reminding me of the endless possibilities that unfold when we remain open to new opportunities and embrace the spirit of inquiry.

The second instance that exemplified the power of the growth mindset for me occurred during a casual evening at a rural pub with a close friend, a finance professor with a natural curiosity about the world. Over a few adult beverages, we found ourselves contemplating the

Chapter Eight: Improvement Doesn't Happen by Chance 147

remarkable cohesion within a particular rural community, especially in the face of challenges. Our curiosity led us to unravel the secrets behind the thriving local ski area (the opposite of big corporate ski resorts), a craft brewery, and a hot springs hotel. The trifecta intrigued us, prompting us to embark on a deep exploration of the unique interplay between these three small enterprises, which we aptly named the "community craft triangle," to explain micro-accountability structures.

In our pursuit of understanding, we unpacked the intricacies of how craft businesses, supported by other local crafts enterprises, create a web of connections that shape how these business owners perceive their ventures and the larger regional context. From our research emerged a pattern of mutual support, small acts of reciprocity, and a genuine commitment to serving others. We heard heartwarming anecdotes, such as the ski resort owner mentoring her staff to treat guests as cherished family members, reminiscent of their own grandparents on a chairlift. Impact, we found, was validated through poignant stories—a guest comparing a brewery's ambiance to his favorite pub in Kerry, Ireland, or a ski resort embracing problem-solving as their unique strength, dubbing it "our jam."

The cohesive spirit of this community stemmed from the strong bonds forged among these craft businesses. The symbiotic relationships were evident, with each entity recognizing the significance of the other in enhancing the overall experience for visitors and locals alike.[6] The owners of Bassett Brewery and Spa Hot Springs Motel emphasized Showdown, the ski resort, as a vital employer and a driving force during winter, while Showdown's owner acknowledged the brewery as a community hub and the motel as a key accommodation choice for visiting skiers.

Beyond the academic revelations, our research journey had an unexpected, delightful consequence—it provided opportunities for quality time with my wife and friends Gary and Sandy, exploring ski resorts, breweries, and hot springs. Amid discussions about our findings, we shared hearty laughs about our skiing escapades, reminisced about past times in Montana, and envisioned future adventures together. Once again, the pursuit of knowledge not only expanded our understanding but also fostered cherished moments with dear friends.

What's even more exciting is the prospect of sharing our discoveries with a wider audience. There's a strong likelihood our research will find a home in an academic journal, allowing us to disseminate our findings and contribute meaningfully to the discourse on community economic development. In essence, our quest for learning not only enriched our academic pursuits but also blessed us with priceless moments of camaraderie and the promise of leaving a lasting impact in the field we explored together.

Action Jackson

In essence, breaking free from narrow-blindedness demands proactive steps. Whether it's moving to a new country or embracing challenges like trying a new sport, starting a garden, or rebuilding a car, learning and personal growth happens as a direct result of the actions we take. So get up and get going. A growth mindset—the desire to learn, the belief in one's ability to learn, and the prioritization of continuous learning—not only fosters happiness but also dispels the noise of narrow-blinded thinking. Those with a growth mindset are perpetual learners, guardians of their health, and champions of change, and are unafraid of leaning into friction. I recall nights in an African truck stop, amid discomfort and mosquito bites, finding solace in the knowledge that I had the opportunity to learn. This overwhelming sense of growth and learning serves as a powerful light, illuminating the path away from narrow-blinded thinking to a life free from contempt.

 A growth mindset stimulates action.

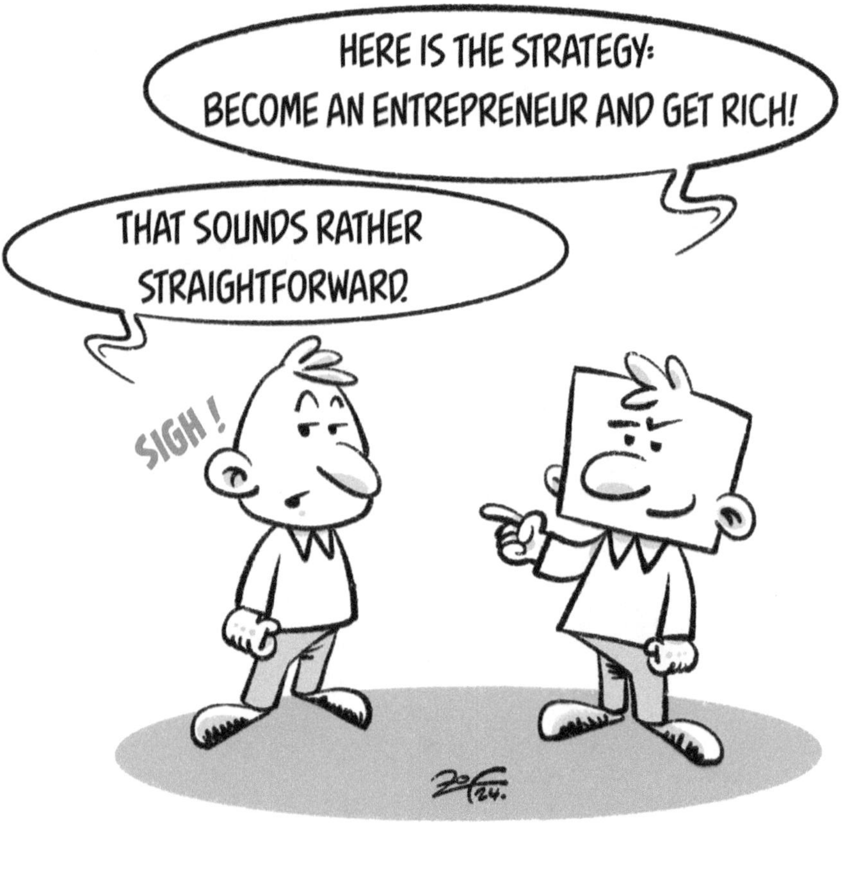
HERE IS THE STRATEGY: BECOME AN ENTREPRENEUR AND GET RICH!
THAT SOUNDS RATHER STRAIGHTFORWARD.
SIGH!

Chapter Nine

From Idea to Action: The Effectuation Way

"Be ready for your opportunity."
—Jamie Foxx

Inventive Resilience: Rising above Contempt

During my travels and work in Australasia, I couldn't help but notice the enthusiasm for innovation prevalent among the citizens. It was striking how people from different parts of the region took immense pride in their country's historical and contemporary inventions. In Japan, my friends and colleagues often emphasized their country's credit for pioneering iconic creations such as the bullet train (Shinkansen), rice cookers, sushi, QR codes, and quartz watches. Similarly, in China, there was a sense of reverence for ancient inventions like paper, tea, gunpowder, and silk, coupled with pride in modern innovations such as flexible TV screens, robotic technologies for infection control, smart glass, and software to predict cardiac arrest. Koreans pointed to a blend of historical achievements such as the mechanical clock and contemporary inventions like educational devices for the blind and advanced medical technologies. The lists are long, perhaps debated, and amazing.

When I ventured to New Zealand, I was surprised by the adventurous and athletic spirit of the Kiwis, reflected in their unique brand of innovation. Locals proudly attributed the origins of commercial bungee jumping, jetpacks, high-speed amphibious vehicles, and even the referee's whistle to their country. Among New Zealand's myriad inventions, one that particularly caught my attention was the Zorb—an inflatable human hamster ball that epitomized the national spirit of adventure. While I marveled at these downhill rolling contraptions, the prospect of trying the Zorb myself left me uncertain. Nonetheless, the variety of innovation landscapes across these regions of the world left a lasting impression, highlighting the rich creativity and ingenuity throughout history and the contemporary ethos. All of these countries seemed to embody the Richard Branson line: "[Business] opportunities are like buses—there's always another one coming."[1]

What is particularly interesting to me is the evolution of these innovations, and the impact they have had on various aspects of our lives, transforming the way we live, travel, experience events, and manage our health. Even more interesting are the instances where countries decide to seize opportunities and face setbacks with resilience—points critical to rebuffing narrow-blinded thinking. Take Ireland, for example. I witnessed a distinct shift toward innovation, especially in the mid-1990s, on the Emerald Isle. The period marked a significant turning point for the country, earning it the moniker of the "Celtic Tiger." The driving force behind this transformation was the influx of major American corporations, which chose to establish their presence in the Republic. The appeal lay in a combination of factors, including low corporate taxation, business-friendly policies, and a young, tech-savvy workforce that made it an attractive destination for international businesses seeking innovation and growth opportunities. Propelled by the strategic decisions of these corporations, Ireland grew rapidly as a nation from the mid-1990s to the early 2000s.

However, Ireland's innovative journey faced a considerable setback when the property bubble burst in early 2009, leading to a major economic downturn. Despite this challenge, the resilience of the Irish people and their adaptability became evident as they navigated through the aftermath, demonstrating the ability to learn from both successes and failures. This period serves as a good roadmap to the dynamic nature of innovation, reflecting not only the opportunities it presents but also the challenges that arise in its wake.

The Irish, like people of other nations, have a history of innovation—and seizing opportunities—worth noting. Their inventive spirit has given birth to a wide array of innovations, from advancements in technology such as color photography, guided torpedoes, and medical inventions like the hypodermic syringe and stethoscope, to significant developments in naval technology like submarines, seat ejectors, and induction coils. To the surprise of many, the Irish can proudly claim credit for the creation of flavored potato chips, adding a touch of culinary creativity to their list of innovations.

Not only are the Irish recognized for their technological contributions, but they also boast a rich literary heritage. The Irish language itself stands as one of the oldest in Europe, with roots dating back to the fourth or fifth century, reflecting the nation's deep cultural history. Throughout the centuries, Ireland has nurtured brilliant literary minds, including iconic figures such as James Joyce, renowned for his groundbreaking works; Edmund Burke, a philosopher and statesman of great influence; Jonathan Swift, whose satirical masterpieces captivated audiences; Oliver Goldsmith, celebrated for his timeless literary classics; Maria Edgeworth, a pioneering novelist; and the incomparable wit of Oscar Wilde and George Bernard Shaw. These luminaries have not only left an indelible mark on Irish literature but have also contributed significantly to the global literary landscape, cementing Ireland's reputation as a hub of literary excellence and creativity.

Putting my obvious bias for Ireland aside, why do all these examples matter? It's evident that each nation's unique history, policies, and societal values play a pivotal role in shaping their approach to innovation. The intricate interplay between culture and innovation underscores the importance of understanding the range of factors that influence a country's inventive landscape, offering valuable insights into the broader global arena of progress and creativity. There is something to be learned here that is applicable to each of us at an individual level, but what?

Innovators move the needle in one way or another and change the way we live, experience life, travel, and attend to our health. Their entrepreneurial spirit calls to mind a poster I once hung in my dorm room during my undergraduate years stating a set of principles known as Peter's Laws.[2] This credo emphasized the importance of action in achieving success. The essence of the message was clear—when faced with a choice, why settle for one option when you can pursue both? Embracing multiple projects often leads to multiple successes. The philosophy advocated for immediate action when something was worth doing, and treated "no" as an opportunity to start afresh at a higher level. It emphasized the idea that persistence pays off; the proactive individual is the one who gets noticed, and the one who does nothing gets replaced. The motto was simple: why walk when you can run?

As I traveled through Australasia and Europe, I was blown away by the number of amazing individuals I met who embodied the principles of what I will call the innovative spirit. Their mindset of seizing opportunities, embracing challenges, and relentlessly pursuing goals was palpable.

Taking action is a choice. If we aspire to combat narrow-blinded thinking and contempt, acquire the mindset of an innovator, and embrace the spirit of self-initiation, we can glean valuable lessons by delving into the insights of renowned innovators across diverse fields and contemplating their methodologies. Exploring the commonalities among these great cultures of innovators provides us with a well-proven route. By discerning shared principles and understanding what can be adapted for use in our own lives, we can navigate through the noise and cultivate a generation of contemporary thinkers and proactive doers.

Chapter Nine: From Idea to Action: The Effectuation Way

Figure 9.1

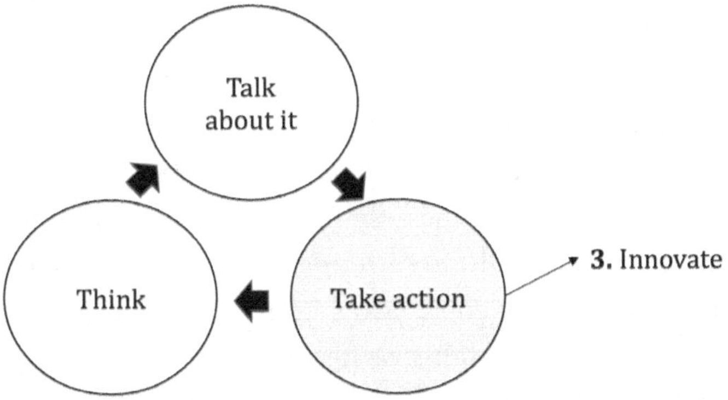

[Diagram: Three circles labeled "Talk about it," "Think," and "Take action" connected in a cycle, with an arrow from "Take action" labeled "3. Innovate"]

Combating narrow-blinded thinking requires innovation.

The Opportunity of Something New

During my stint as a research fellow at the Max Planck Institute of Economics in Germany, I had the privilege of delving into two groundbreaking ideas spearheaded by exceptional scholars. The first of these concepts aimed to tackle the enigmatic question of what exactly constitutes an "opportunity," while the second introduced me to a fascinating concept known as "effectuation."

Around the turn of the millennium, academia was abuzz with efforts to demystify the intricate realm of entrepreneurship. Prior to this, discussions surrounding entrepreneurship were rife, but a cohesive body of research on the subject had yet to coalesce. This all changed when two visionary researchers, Scott Shane and Sankaran Venkataraman, set out to construct a framework for comprehending the multifaceted entrepreneurial landscape.[3] Their research primarily focused on understanding the essence of opportunities—why they come into existence, and the factors influencing whether individuals seize or overlook them.

In my exploration of Shane and Venkataraman's research, several key insights stood out. First and foremost, entrepreneurship hinged on individuals harboring distinctive beliefs. One of those beliefs is a deep-seated conviction that they possessed the capability to transform available resources into something of greater value. Belief in oneself aside, it became apparent that people possessed varying levels of information, which significantly impacted their ability to identify opportunities. Additionally, even if one possessed the acumen to discern opportunities, they could falter in the execution phase due to a failure to act on their insights or perceive new means-end relationships. In essence, entrepreneurship emerged as a multifaceted endeavor encompassing the triad of three important elements: opportunity recognition, opportunity evaluation, and opportunity exploitation.[4]

These insights from Shane and Venkataraman's research not only shed light on the essence of entrepreneurship but also on the intricate web of factors that underlie an individual's journey to recognize, assess, and ultimately harness opportunities. In the vast body of research around entrepreneurship, these revelations were pivotal in unveiling the mysteries long shrouded in this dynamic field of study.

An alternative perspective of entrepreneurship emerged in the early 2000s, one that described an intricate relationship between innovation, opportunity, and entrepreneurship. It was pioneered by the distinguished scholar Saras Sarasvathy, whose seminal work introduced the contrasting concepts of causation and effectuation.[5] Sarasvathy's groundbreaking insights provided a fresh lens through which to view decision-making strategy in the entrepreneurial realm.

In Sarasvathy's illuminating framework, entrepreneurship is intricately interwoven with the idea of strategy. When faced with a decision involving an opportunity, such as determining the price of a product, entrepreneurs often draw upon the existing economic or marketing strategies to guide their choices. This strategic approach, referred to as causation, implies decisions are influenced by predetermined goals and an analysis of cause-and-effect relationships. Entrepreneurs employing causation tend to follow established paths, relying on market research and predetermined plans to shape their strategies.

Contrastingly, effectuation, as proposed by Sarasvathy, signifies a radically different approach to entrepreneurship and indeed decision-making. Entrepreneurs employing effectual reasoning do not start with specific goals or preconceived plans. Instead, they begin by assessing their available means—such as skills, resources, and networks—and then explore the myriad of possibilities these elements afford. This approach embraces uncertainty and views challenges as opportunities for creative problem-solving. Effectual thinkers leverage the surprises and contingencies that emerge, adapting their strategies based on the evolving circumstances and using their resources flexibly.

Sarasvathy offers this example to explain the difference between the two approaches: "All the chef needs to do is list the ingredients needed, shop for them, and then actually cook the meal." This is a causation approach. However, another way of thinking about opportunity and entrepreneurship is by saying, "Here is what I have, now what can I do with it?" Returning to the chef example, Sarasvathy says, "In the second case, the host asks the chef to look through the cupboards in the kitchen for possible ingredients and utensils and then cook a meal. Here, the chef has to imagine possible menus based on the given ingredients and utensils, select the menu, and then prepare the meal. This is a process of effectuation. It begins with given ingredients and utensils and focuses on preparing one of many possible desirable meals with them."[6]

Sarasvathy's work thus highlights the nuanced decision-making processes that underpin entrepreneurial action. By juxtaposing causation and effectuation, her research offers valuable insights into how entrepreneurs can successfully navigate the dynamic challenges of opportunity assessment and exploitation. Effectuation, with its emphasis on adaptability and creativity, encourages entrepreneurs to view uncertainty as a canvas upon which they can paint innovative solutions. This approach not only fosters resilience but also empowers entrepreneurs to navigate the complex and ever-changing landscape of the business world, paving the way for transformative and sustainable ventures. As entrepreneurs continue to grapple with the challenges of the modern marketplace, Sarasvathy's paradigm offers a compelling framework that encourages them to embrace uncertainty, think creatively, and forge innovative pathways toward success.

But why delve into all this? By understanding different approaches to opportunities and their outcomes, we can better shape our individual approach to thinking through problems, making decisions, and translating those decisions to action. The way we perceive opportunities, and subsequently, how we interpret and respond to their outcomes, can impact narrow-blinded thinking and reduce contempt. Moreover, understanding these contrasting approaches to innovation is essential not just for entrepreneurs but also for policymakers, educators, and business leaders. It informs the way we design solutions to education programs, craft business policies, and mentor aspiring thinkers.

Who's Your Inventor?

The entrepreneurial mindset is contagious and can be both shared and learned. For example, Elon Musk's formative years were spent in the milieu of Pretoria, South Africa, where some would suggest the entrepreneurial spirit permeated his upbringing. Born into a family that epitomized versatility, Musk was influenced by his predecessors' layers of diverse expertise. His father was not only an accomplished engineer but also a skilled pilot, seasoned sailor, and astute consultant. Moreover, his father's ownership of a mine underscored the family's multifaceted engagement with industry.

Not only was his father an exemplar of entrepreneurial spirit, his grandfather before him was an intrepid traveler and undertook daring journeys, including once flying the family to Australia in a single-engine plane. Such stories illustrate a legacy of audacity and ambition.

It's a mindset. My guess is this family's entrepreneurial spirit impacted Elon's processes of founding and/or spearheading companies like PayPal, SpaceX, Starlink, Tesla, Open AI, and X (formerly Twitter). Each of these ventures has reshaped their respective industries, from online finance to space exploration, electric vehicles, satellite communication, and artificial intelligence.

When speaking of innovators whose work has had impact across multiple industries, it's impossible not to mention Sir Richard Branson, the visionary British entrepreneur who stands at the helm of a conglomerate controlling more than 250 companies. From record labels and megastores to airlines, rail groups, and even venturing into the realms of space travel and tourism, Branson has left a permanent mark on the global business landscape. Remarkably, he has also personally experienced the vast expanse of space, underscoring his boundless aspirations.

Born to a barrister and a former ballet dancer, Branson's upbringing included a blend of refinement and artistic flair. As a young private school student, he encountered skepticism from his headmaster, who famously predicted Branson would either end up in prison or ascend to millionaire status. Contrary to these prognostications, Branson defied the odds.

His journey to success was fraught with challenges both personal and financial, including dyslexia and some precarious business ventures. Despite these obstacles, he not only overcame but soared to unimaginable heights, achieving billionaire status. The story of Sir Richard Branson is a testament to resilience, innovation, and the transformative power of relentless pursuit, embodying the spirit of the entrepreneur who defies expectations and redefines the possibilities of success.

If these two stories fail to inspire you to adopt an effectual entrepreneurial mindset, then I find myself at a loss for words. The willingness to innovate and act could make you rich and famous, but first and most importantly, it is an antidote to narrow-blinded thinking. To be clear, an innovator does not need to achieve household-name status. You don't need to be an icon like Elon Musk, Richard Branson, Steve Jobs, Mark Zuckerberg, Oprah Winfrey, or Bill Gates. Nor must you possess a compelling narrative like the story of Ray Kroc, who weathered multiple failures before mortgaging his home to acquire a relatively unknown fast-food company from the McDonald brothers in 1961, subsequently transforming it into the most successful fast-food corporation in the world.

I staunchly contend innovation can happen in the most subtle and non-iconic ways. It is taking the first step. It is simply a courageous decision to act and try something new. It is working with what you have at hand. Whatever happens after, I say let the cards drop how they will. Consider the likes of Richard Dawkins and Christopher Hitchens, scholars who, through keen recognition, evaluation, and exploitation of opportunities, initiated global conversations on evolution, religion, and critical self-reflective logic. Their innovative thinking and intellectual contributions wield an influence that rivals, if not surpasses, traditional business success. Or take Joe Rogan, who recognized, evaluated, and seized the opportunity to host open and uncensored debates with intriguing personalities on his podcasts. These individuals are not merely successful in the traditional business sense, but they are innovators of thought, challenging norms and shaping the intellectual landscape. They possess the acumen to identify problems and the courage to implement transformative solutions. In essence, the entrepreneur extends beyond the conventional business realm, encompassing those who revolutionize thinking and contribute meaningfully to the broader intellectual discourse through opportunity recognition, opportunity evaluation, and opportunity exploitation.

Daily Successes through Small Decisions

The media often romanticizes the idea of an entrepreneur. I must admit, I've been guilty of perpetuating the same narrative in this book. Despite this, we can learn a lot from these individuals' examples beyond their fame; they are people who are willing to try the seemingly new in hope of finding a solution or more fertile ground. Does it always work? Nope. Failure will come. Must you have a definitive strategy or end game in mind? Also no. As was pointed out earlier, research has suggested we all can have multiple means as well as multiple ends—through some version of recognizing, evaluating, and exploiting opportunities. Thus, it sometimes requires us to say maybe there is another way of doing things. This too is taking action. And guess what? You don't have to be famous to do any of this. Success is not guaranteed, and setbacks are inevitable. However, these setbacks, often labeled as failures, should be viewed as invaluable opportunities for refining and enhancing one's thinking.

The true essence of entrepreneurial spirit lies not in flawless success stories but in the resilience to confront challenges, the openness to explore alternative paths, and the determination to view setbacks as stepping stones toward personal and professional growth. I am reminded of this entrepreneurial mindset when I think of my two dear friends Dylan and Tara, who gave up their jobs in Canada as a city planner and a high school teacher, respectively. They sold everything, moved to Turks and Caicos, and started a paint business on the island. About eight years later, it has now grown to include several other businesses. A prime example of opportunity recognition, evaluation, and most importantly, exploitation! These experiences, whether recognized by the public or not, form the crucible of an individual's journey toward a more innovative and adaptable mindset.

Take Your Own Advice

Have you ever noticed how in academia the little thing called effectuation seems to be in short supply? Professors, bless their strategic souls, often find themselves trapped in the clutches of the one-size-fits-all shoe when it comes to education. But hey, we all know education is more of a funky, multi-patterned sock and retro-shoed kind of affair, right?

Many of us have experienced it firsthand. Picture a near-retired professor, a person who has been using the same lecture material since the dawn of the floppy disk. This eccentric character got a kick out of being the toughest professor in town, curving grades like a mad genius, all in the name of pushing students to conquer their exams. Students, on their end, had nothing nice to say. Is this the person you would learn from?

Now imagine a different kind of character, a carnival of engagement and challenge. In their lectures and office hours, there's novelty around every corner. No more snoozing through PowerPoint marathons in class—oh no. Hopefully, you have been fortunate to have at least one educator like this. As a faculty member, I am striving for option #2.

What's my point? The courage to try something new can breathe life into any job, even academia. Opportunities to shake things up and do things differently are like daily specials at a quirky cafe—they're right in front of us, begging to be tasted. We just need to decide to recognize, evaluate, and exploit them. These are the innovations that can spice up our lives—new patterns, practices, or forms of taking action. Go on, give it a whirl! Who knows, you might just stumble upon the academic version of disco socks and retro kicks.

The Everyday Entrepreneur

Engaging with what I call entrepreneurial business owners is an intense privilege. When I speak of entrepreneurs, I'm referring to individuals who chart their own course using the resources at hand. Take, for instance, WestPaw Design in Montana, a manufacturing company specializing in pet products. What sets them apart is an unwavering commitment to the B Corps ethos—centered on balancing profits, people, and the planet. In the competitive landscape, WestPaw continually explores, evaluates, and exploits new ideas to maintain their presence in this dynamic industry.

There is also the inspiring story of TenTree International, born in Saskatchewan through the vision of two friends. Their unique model involves selling a T-shirt with the promise to plant ten trees for each purchase. The success of this eco-conscious venture is evident as they expand into diverse markets.

Another noteworthy example comes from two friends in Canada addressing the age-old issue of smelly hockey gear. Collaborating with a Korean patent holder, they've introduced products with nanocleaning properties, revolutionizing the sports equipment market.

Not to be overlooked is the owner of a local espresso bar situated in downtown Charlottetown, Prince Edward Island, Canada. In a caffeine-saturated battleground with eleven coffee establishments in a two-block radius, including the behemoth Starbucks, this entrepreneur has risen triumphant, offering a unique and distinctive coffee experience for more than a decade. Each of these entrepreneurial tales exemplifies resilience, innovation, and a commitment to making a difference, showcasing the diverse and inspiring landscape of entrepreneurial endeavors.

In preceding chapters, I highlight the remarkable ski resort CEOs with whom I've collaborated in the past—truly exceptional entrepreneurs in a highly competitive and risky industry. For example, ski resorts are often reliant on a narrow window of three to four months, sometimes less with the unpredictability of weather and snowfall, to make their yearly profits. Facing climate and marketplace instability, the industry has undergone substantial transformations in the last two decades. Notably, changes have included substantial investments in snowmaking, the consolidation of ski resorts, and strategic alignment, all in response to Vail Resorts' dominant position. The strategic introduction of mega-passes like Epic and Ikon has resulted in a significant oligopoly, consolidating power across major ski markets nationwide.

Yet, amid this industry evolution, there remain crafty entrepreneurs who embody the spirit of individuality. Take the owners of Maverick Mountain who manage with only one year-round employee—the owner himself, a true jack-of-all-trades. Similarly, in September 2020, Katie Boedecker took the reins of Showdown Montana from her father, George Willett, who had owned and operated it for an impressive forty-seven years. These stories of individual and family-driven ski ventures underscore the diverse and resilient fabric of the ski resort industry.

Some may look at the everyday industries these entrepreneurs inhabit and call them innovators of the ordinary. But that is not at all the case. They are maestros of action. They are set apart by their commitment to rising early every morning and working late into every evening. Their work extends beyond mere operational logistics; it's an orchestrated effort to cultivate daily operations that not only forge stronger human bonds but also deliver bespoke experiences to their customers. Operating with a unique mindset, they navigate each decision with a profound understanding of the given means at their disposal, leveraging them to achieve multiple ends. In doing so, they strive to connect with customers, establish their individual definition of success, and provide an authentically crafted experience—a remarkable feat in a field where success is often associated with a willingness to act.

The Entrepreneurial Bell

Do you hear the calling to be a bit more entrepreneurial? During my visit to Cape Breton in Canada, I made a stop at the Alexander Graham Bell Museum. Bell, a lifelong inventor best known for inventing and patenting the first telephone, went on to establish the American Telephone and Telegraph Company (now widely recognized as AT&T). As I strolled through the rooms of this charming museum, I came across a quote, spoken by Bell himself, that encapsulates the essence of entrepreneurship, resilience, and the imperative of taking action: "The inventor . . . looks upon the world and is not contented with things as they are. He wants to improve whatever he sees, he wants to benefit the world; he is haunted by an idea. The spirit of invention possesses him, seeking materialization."[7] This quote has stuck with me for years.

Combatting narrow-blindedness and contempt requires action from people who want to improve themselves and those around them through the discovery of new patterns, practices, or forms of organizing. In my own life, seemingly modest decisions, like saying yes to the idea of initiating a case competition program or running a volunteer tax program, have yielded remarkable outcomes. We've encountered a number of entrepreneurs along this journey, and what's intriguing about all of them is their collective sense of adventure, kindness, and an unwavering passion for setting out into the unknown. They possess the ability to recognize, evaluate, and exploit opportunities, driving a narrative of innovation and forward momentum.

 **Say goodbye to narrow-blinded thinking by exploiting opportunities with unwavering persistence.**

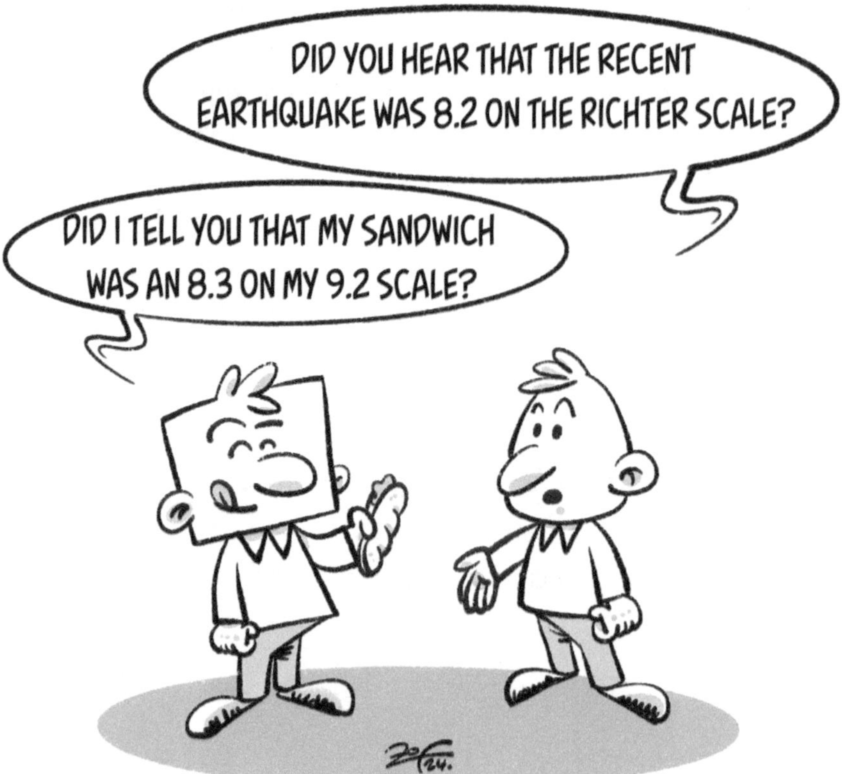
DID YOU HEAR THAT THE RECENT EARTHQUAKE WAS 8.2 ON THE RICHTER SCALE?
DID I TELL YOU THAT MY SANDWICH WAS AN 8.3 ON MY 9.2 SCALE?

Conclusion

Brace for Impact

"Don't ever underestimate the impact that
you may have on someone else's life."
—**Anonymous**

The Peaks and Valleys of Our Mountains

Between the giants of India and China, Nepal is a compact South Asian nation boasting a population of around thirty million with diverse topography encompassing lush, forested hills, expansive plains, and some of the most breathtaking mountains in the world. It is perhaps best known for the Himalayan Mountain range, which hosts the iconic Mount Everest, the world's highest peak, and Napal's capital city, Kathmandu, a bustling hub for approximately two million residents.

The significant variations in elevation in Nepal contribute to a spectrum of temperature zones, giving rise to Nepal's unique five seasons: the traditional quartet of winter, spring, summer, and fall, plus the distinctive monsoon season, characterized by heavy rainfall.

Also significant in Nepal are the stark levels of inequality. According to data from the UNESCO Institute for Statistics, although 67.9 percent of Nepalese adults exhibit basic literacy, a glaring gender gap persists. Notably, eight out of ten males are literate, in contrast to only six out of ten women who share this fundamental skill. Despite a relatively high attendance rate for primary school, where most children complete up to grade five, only 60 percent continue up to grade twelve, and less than 12 percent proceed to tertiary education. These alarming numbers unveil a systemic barrier to higher learning.

Despite the constitutional guarantee of free general education, inadequate financial allocation from the national budget hampers the implementation of an effective education system, eroding the citizens' trust in the Nepalese government. This skepticism was exemplified by a no-confidence vote against the federal government in 2021.

Beyond federal funding challenges, Nepal grapples with pervasive issues such as food insecurity, limited access to education, and a burdensome load of daily living expenses, including those for social or religious festivities and health costs. Widespread cultural acceptance of child labor creates fertile ground for traffickers, particularly as families in extreme poverty, grappling with rising unemployment, encourage their children to contribute to the family's survival, rendering them vulnerable to exploitation.

These socioeconomic factors give rise to a deeply entrenched system of forced labor. The insidious cycle typically begins with subtle recruitment tactics that progressively escalate into overt threats, violence, and exploitation. The system is perpetuated as individuals are coerced into working against their will, gripped by the fear of severe penalties or threats of punishment should they attempt to break free.

Trafficking, a nefarious form of forced labor, tends to fester in communities located in remote, isolated areas grappling with extreme poverty. Traffickers prey on families burdened by poverty and debt, exploiting the vulnerabilities created by weak legal systems and limited governmental protections. While exploitation can occur visibly among marginalized or discriminated individuals, those residing in remote regions face heightened risks, as traffickers strategically elude labor regulators by isolating their victims in secluded private settings.

The intricate interplay of socio-economic, cultural, legislative, and topographic factors in Nepal creates an environment ripe for traffickers to exploit vulnerable individuals, treating them as commodities for financial gain, callously disregarding their fundamental human dignity and rights. Children, tragically, bear the brunt of this exploitation, with one in three trafficking victims globally being children under the age of twelve. Young girls, in particular, find themselves in perilous forced labor situations, making them susceptible to sexual exploitation. The United Nations Office on Drugs and Crime (UNODC) reveals the distressing reality that these girls are sold to future exploiters for amounts ranging from USD $600 to USD $3,000 in the sex trade. Disturbingly, over half of the victims trafficked globally come from the region around Nepal.

A Game Changer

Strides are being taken to address the pressing issue of trafficking in Nepal. Illustrating this commitment is the inclusion of anti-trafficking initiatives in the United Nations' Sustainable Development Goals (SDGs), which further offer the ambitious objective of attaining gender equality and empowering all women and girls by 2030. However, it's crucial to dispel the notion that transformative change and impact solely stem from large organizations like the United Nations. The landscape of progress is more nuanced and diverse.

An example of passionate, grassroots impact is an organization called Tsering's Fund (TF).[1] TF has made substantial strides in improving the lives of underprivileged and at-risk Nepalese girls through educational sponsorships, medical care, and basic living assistance. TF operates with a clear mission: to make a personal and tangible difference in the lives of these girls. By leveraging funds from private donors and adhering to a principle of maximizing every dollar raised, TF has been effective at addressing the child trafficking problem in Nepal.

Since its inception, TF has garnered millions of dollars from a generous pool of some 600 benefactors. Their financial support has been instrumental in safeguarding at-risk girls and women in the Helambu region of Nepal from falling victim to trafficking, thereby preventing the associated risks of sexual exploitation, poverty, and premature death. TF's impactful initiatives extend to 400 sponsored grade-school girls; 30 young women pursuing higher education in disciplines such as nursing, law, dentistry, and accounting; and 110 orphans residing in orphanages. In addition to covering their tuition, TF goes above and beyond by funding essential boarding and living expenses for these individuals, ensuring a comprehensive and sustained approach to their well-being.

At a certain juncture, the CEO of TF enlisted my assistance in evaluating the impact of his organization. To tackle this, my co-researchers and I adopted two distinct approaches. First and foremost, we endeavored to measure impact in a manner conducive to comparing nonprofit organizations.[2] We posed a fundamental question: is it time to enhance tax-exempt nonprofit reporting for the explicit purpose of assessing impact? The inquiry stems from the observation that US tax-exempt nonprofits consistently lag in terms of reporting, communicating, and facilitating comparisons of the value they generate, particularly concerning sustainability and impact. Using TF as a case study, our exploration demonstrated how entities could recalibrate their approach to enable a measurable, objective, and verifiable assessment of impact in practice. Our findings affirmed that not only is this achievable, but it is also imperative. If nonprofits benefit from tax exemptions across various dimensions, there should be heightened scrutiny and disclosure mechanisms in place for comparing and assessing their impact. Oversight and comparative analyses are pivotal in ensuring accountability and transparency within the nonprofit sector, especially given the substantial tax privileges granted to these organizations.

Taking my investigation a step further, I collaborated with another research group to engage families, students, teachers, and community members associated with TF in Nepal. Our aim was to gain insights into how they conceptualized and measured impact. The responses we received were exceptionally enlightening. Participants articulated a myriad of constraints in their lives, encompassing economic challenges, time constraints, familial conflicts, poor infrastructure, and cultural and health issues. These constraints formed the backdrop against which they understood the concept of impact.[3]

Interestingly, the people we interviewed in Nepal framed their "duty" to TF as an integral part of the impact assessment process, akin to the notion of accountability. In interviews, the participants emphasized their duty to TF as their contribution to impact because, through TF's support, their children received education, they gained structure to channel their efforts, they had local champions serving as mentors, they could harmonize traditional and contemporary cultural practices, and their overall health was bolstered. For them, fulfilling this duty became a driving force for impact within the community, exemplifying a form of community-driven governance in steering the impact process.

What is the point here? The essence of effecting positive change demands more than mere contemplation; it necessitates deliberate thought, proactive dialogue, and decisive action. Anchored in the 3 Ts—think, talk about it, and take action—and their symbiotic sub-components, this model operates concertedly to eliminate narrow-blindedness and contempt. In doing so it helps people, leaders, and companies skillfully navigate the vessel of impact toward meaningful destinations. In essence, it is a call, urging you to embrace a purposeful mindset, engage in purposeful conversations, and embark on purposeful actions, thus forging a pathway toward substantial and enduring impact.

Figure 10.1

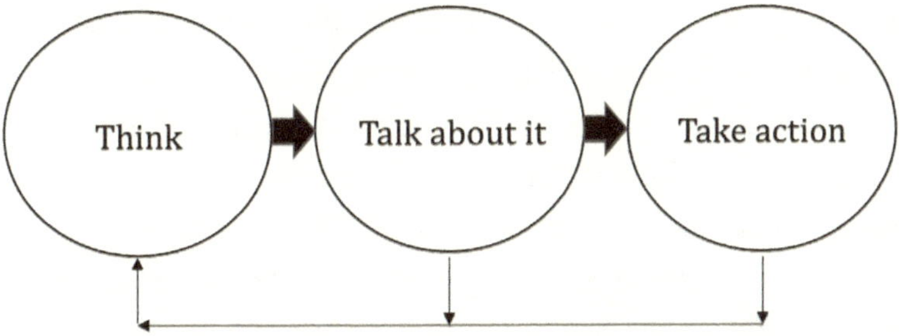

Think → Talk about it → Take action

Impact emerges from a process that reduces narrow-blinded thinking and contempt.

Impact Is Measured in Many Ways

In South America, I collaborated with a dear friend to delve into the realm of impact measurement in a context where such practices were not yet well established.[4] Commissioned by a national government that was struggling with how to allocate entrepreneurial grants in the absence of a consistent and objective system, our research aimed to explore the foundations of impact measurement, its application, and how it shaped behaviors—particularly in a region where preconceived notions of impact measurement were scarce.

Over two years, we engaged with numerous entrepreneurs venturing into the development and use of formalized impact measurement approaches. What emerged was a practical application: entrepreneurs were leveraging impact measurement to showcase and communicate their progress to others. Their rationale was clear—they wanted to provide evidence of their impact in order to enhance decision-making, refine management practices, establish legitimacy, and gain access to resources. In this emerging geography, impact measurement was not just a tool; it was a means of accountability, an approach that resonated with the practical realities of the business world.

However, a surprising revelation surfaced—a critical fracture or misunderstanding in the concept of impact measurement, prevalent not only in South America but also in many developed nations. This paradox revolved around the divergent understandings of impact and measurement. Here is what we learned. Entrepreneurs were constructing arguments to demonstrate their impact and importance (arguments for worth), but simultaneously found themselves compelled to measure and craft arguments for their relevance to external entities (arguments for legitimacy). The discovery shed light on the multifaceted nature of impact—one that is personally meaningful, observable, and reportable. As we discuss impact and measurement in this chapter, it becomes evident that impact wears different hats, each holding significance based on individual perspectives and organizational needs. Which dimension of impact resonates with you?

It's not surprising that industry-wide impact measurement techniques and practices are greeted with enthusiasm, with organizations pioneering cost-benefit ratio methodologies for social programs. However, our eye-opening experience in South America illuminated a nuanced reality: impact and its measurement are far from one-size-fits-all. The awareness that impact and measurement serve multiple purposes is a crucial step in deciphering the diverse approaches entrepreneurs (be they social, profit-driven, or hybrid-oriented) employ to articulate their significance. This holds true for individuals as well.

The underlying point is that the intricate construction of impact narratives and the methodologies used to measure them inspire further exploration of how to seamlessly integrate the experiential with the objective world of measures in innovative and creative ways. In essence, understanding the dynamic relationship between impact and its measurement is not just about embracing industry-wide practices but recognizing the need for tailored, nuanced approaches to align with diverse goals and perspectives. You can be the architect of your impact.

The End of Narrow-Blinded Thinking

At the heart of this book lies a powerful concept: nine strategies to weed out narrow-blinded thinking, that pervasive mindset that takes root in our thought processes, infiltrates our conversations, and thrives in the absence of action. In a landscape increasingly marred by the dismissive notion of "they are wrong or they are the problem," where diverse views are summarily deemed worthless without earnest consideration of the underlying logic, this contemptuous approach chokes thinking, stifles constructive dialogue, and paralyzes meaningful action. Its corrosive influence spreads like dandelion seeds, impeding progress across a spectrum of challenges that are, at their core, surmountable. So, the paramount question remains: how can we usher in meaningful impact in the face of such destructive patterns of thought, speech, and inaction?

Simply and carefully defining the topic at hand is a great start toward combating our illusions of knowledge and comprehending our true perception. Practicing the principles of evidence-informed thinking is the next step as we consider ethics, stakeholder concerns, practitioner expertise, local data, and experimental insights alongside formal research findings. Reflection follows as we consider, question, and meditate to draw out meaningful insights. We must then remove the blinders of groupthink, asking instead, "Where might I be wrong?" and, in turn, counteracting our overconfidence, asking questions, and opening opportunities for deeper exploration. As we confront challenges, we can explain ourselves more effectively. As thoughts and discussion comes together, we can harness the power of action to obliterate narrow-blinded thinking and contempt. Small wins and a growth mindset add up to tangible outcomes, the catalyst for meaningful change, accomplishment, and empowerment. Action, often synonymous with entrepreneurship and innovation, then unleashes our efforts to recognize, evaluate, and exploit opportunities effectively.

Unified under the banner of the 3Ts—think, talk about it, and take action—these elements converge to form an open-minded powerhouse within the pages of this book. Together, they don't just diminish but have the transformative potential to obliterate narrow-blinded thinking and, in tandem, quell contempt. In the harmonious orchestration of these components, the true potential for impactful change emerges. It is not merely a theoretical framework but a practical guide, a new roadmap to not only mitigate the frivolous but to instigate a profound shift. It is through the deployment of the 3Ts that the journey toward authentic, meaningful impact takes its resolute first steps.

Figure 10.2

Talk
about it
1. The dark side of groups
2. The problem with overconfidence
3. How to explain your position
1. The illusion of
knowledge
2. Evidence-informed
decision-making
3. Reflect
Think
Take action
1. Experiment
2. A growth mindset
3. Innovate

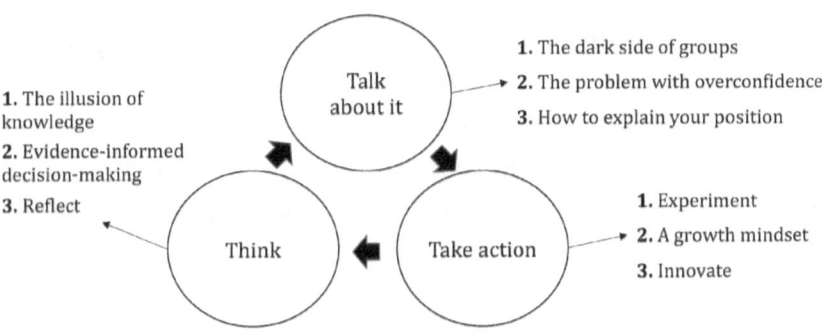

The end of narrow-blinded thinking and contempt.

The age-old wisdom that you can't manage what you don't measure has long been a staple in business school teachings, emphasizing the critical role of measurement in comprehending and steering impact. While there is some truth to this adage, my journeys around the world, particularly in South America, Africa, and Asia, have revealed a nuanced tension between the concepts of impact and measurement—underscoring the question of "for whom?" and "for what purpose?" This tension surfaced as people and organizations grapple with articulating their significance both internally and to external stakeholders.

After over a decade immersed in contemplation and discourse on narrow-blinded thinking and contempt, I've come to view the notion of impact very differently. By adopting the 3T approach—thinking, talking about it, and taking action—you can, and will, undergo a positive shift and therefore have an impact. However you choose to measure it is up to you, but do try to engage in impact assessment.

The potential for impact awaits you—brace yourself for its arrival! As I reflect on personal experiences, whether it's my apprehension while swimming with sharks or the fear I felt as a boa constrictor draped around my neck, I can say profound impact requires embracing discomfort. When we settle into an uncomfortable zone, we are also probably expanding as a people. As you embark on this transformative journey to eradicate narrow-blinded thinking, I hope you commit wholeheartedly to the principles laid out in this book. Let your imagination run wild. In doing so, you'll not only successfully navigate the discomfort of growth but also revel in the potential for a truly transformative impact waiting to be unleashed. Best of luck to you on your new route!

Acknowledgments

TO MY BELOVED WIFE, JANET. For more than two decades, you have been the unwavering pillar supporting all my endeavors. Our journey together has been filled with incredible adventures across the globe, many of which find their place within the pages of this book. Words fall short in capturing the depth of my gratitude to you.

To my wonderful parents, Esther and Eamon, I consider myself incredibly fortunate to have won the parental lottery with you both. Your wisdom, guidance, and the valuable lessons you've imparted have shaped me into the person I am today.

To the phenomenal team at Greenleaf Book Group. Embarking on the literary journey with a seasoned crew like yours is a stroke of good fortune. You're not just professionals; you're virtuosos! A special nod to my editor extraordinaire, Lee—your guidance and saint-like tolerance throughout the manuscript's evolution deserve a standing ovation, or better yet, a book dedicated solely to your heroic feats.

And last but certainly not least, to my good buddy Doug Fletcher. How I'm lucky enough to have a pal who's not only a two-time best-selling author but also willing to put up with my questionable jokes is another of life's great mysteries. Your friendship and mentorship were the secret sauce in getting this book to where it is. Thank you for being in my corner.

Notes

Preface

1. Steinbeck, John. *Travels with Charley in Search of America*. Penguin Classics Deluxe Edition. New York: Penguin, 2012.

Introduction

1. Schriber, Roberta A., Joanne M. Chung, Katherine S. Sorensen, and Richard W. Robins. "Dispositional Contempt: A First Look at the Contemptuous Person." *Journal of Personality and Social Psychology* 113, no. 2 (2017): 280.
2. Haidt, Jonathan. *The Happiness Hypothesis: Finding Modern Truth in Ancient Wisdom*. New York: Basic Books, 2006.
3. Brooks, Arthur C. "Opinion | Our Culture of Contempt." *New York Times*, March 4, 2019, https://www.nytimes.com/2019/03/02/opinion/sunday/political-polarization.html.

Chapter 1

1. "About the Sector | Imagine Canada." n.d., https://www.imaginecanada.ca/en/About-the-sector.
2. Stuart, Reginald. "Ford Orders Recall of 1.5 Million Pintos for Safety Changes." *New York Times*, June 10, 1978, https://www.nytimes.com/1978/06/10/archives/ford-orders-recall-of-15-million-pintos-for-safety-changes-inquiry.html.
3. Fernbach, Philip M., Todd Rogers, Craig R. Fox, and Steven A. Sloman. "Political Extremism Is Supported by an Illusion of Understanding." *Psychological Science* 24, no. 6 (2013): 939–946.
4. Gamble, Edward N., Timothy J. Rupert, and Anne L. Christensen. "Can Tax Policy Choice Architecture Motivate Positive Climate Change Actions?" Working paper, 2024.
5. Gamble, Edward N., Andreas Thorsen, and Laura Black. "Expanding Strategic Opportunities in Nonprofits: Mapping the Interdependencies of Critical Performance Variables." *Nonprofit and Voluntary Sector Quarterly* 48, no. 3 (2019): 616–632.

6. Gamble, Edward N., and Pablo Muñoz. "When Tax-Exempt Nonprofits Detract Value from Society." *Academy of Management Perspectives* 36, no. 1 (2022): 50–92.

Chapter 2

1. Center for Evidence-Based Management (CEBMa). http://www.cebma.org.
2. Gamble, Edward N., and R. Blake Jelley. "The Case for Competition: Learning About Evidence-Based Management through Case Competition." *Academy of Management Learning & Education* 13, no. 3 (2014): 433–445.
3. "SIWI – Leading Expert in Water Governance." n.d., https://siwi.org/stockholm-water-prize/laureates/2023-professor-andrea-rinaldo.
4. Peterson, Jordan B. *12 Rules for Life: An Antidote to Chaos*. Toronto: Random House Canada, 2018.
5. Gamble and Jelley, "The Case for Competition," 433–445.

Chapter 3

1. Buettner, Dan. *The Blue Zones: 9 Lessons for Living Longer from the People Who've Lived the Longest*. National Geographic Books, 2012.
2. Rowling, J. K. *Harry Potter and the Goblet of Fire*. New York: Scholastic, 2002.
3. "Reflective Writing: What Is Reflection? Why Do It?" University of Hull Library, January 19, 2024, https://libguides.hull.ac.uk/reflectivewriting/reflection1a.
4. Higginson, Thomas Wentworth. *The Works of Epictetus: Consisting of His Discourses, in Four Books, the Enchiridion, and Fragments*. BoD–Books on Demand, 2022.
5. Hegel, Georg Wilhelm Friedrich. "Introduction: Reason in History." In *Lectures on the Philosophy of World History*. Translated by H. B. Nisbet. Cambridge University Press, 1975.
6. Reik, Theodor. *Curiosities of the Self: Illusions We Have About Ourselves*. New York: Farrar, Straus & Giroux, 1965.
7. Gamble, Edward N., and Haley A. Beer. "Spiritually Informed Not-for-Profit Performance Measurement." *Journal of Business Ethics* 141 (2017): 451–468.
8. Chu, Li-Chuan. "The Benefits of Meditation Vis-à-Vis Emotional Intelligence, Perceived Stress and Negative Mental Health." *Stress and Health: Journal of the International Society for the Investigation of Stress* 26, no. 2 (2010): 169–180.
9. Chu, "The Benefits of Meditation," 169–180.
10. Frankl, Viktor E. *Man's Search for Meaning*. New York: Simon and Schuster, 1985.

Chapter 4

1. "Cult," *Oxford English Dictionary*, accessed May 3, 2024, https://www.oed.com/dictionary/cult_n?tab=factsheet#7736881.
2. Bill D'Elia, dir. Chris D'Elia: *White Male. Black Comic*. New York: Comedy Central, 2013.
3. Gamble and Beer, "Spiritually Informed Not-for-Profit Performance Measurement," 451–468.
4. Angelovski, Ivan, Timothy Sawa, and Mark Kelley. "Mormon Church in Canada Moved $1B out of the Country Tax Free—and It's Legal." CBC, October 27, 2022, https://www.cbc.ca/news/canada/mormon-church-jesus-christ-latter-day-saints-funds-charity-1.6630190.
5. Whyte, William H., Jr. "Groupthink." *Fortune*, March 1952, 114–117, 142, 146.
6. Janis, Irving L., and Leon Mann. *Decision Making: A Psychological Analysis of Conflict, Choice, and Commitment*. New York: Free Press, 1977.
7. Haidt, Jonathan. *The Happiness Hypothesis: Finding Modern Truth in Ancient Wisdom*. Basic Books, 2006.
8. Haidt, *The Happiness Hypothesis*, 60.
9. "Business for Good." B Lab United States & Canada, 2024, https://usca.bcorporation.net/.
10. Parker, Simon C., Edward N. Gamble, Peter W. Moroz, and Oana Branzei. "The Impact of B Lab Certification on Firm Growth." *Academy of Management Discoveries* 5, no. 1 (2019): 57–77.
11. Gamble, Edward N., and Gary Caton. "Pulling Back the Curtain of Environmental Accountability: How Boundaries Shape Environmental Identities in the Ski Industry." *Accounting, Auditing & Accountability Journal* (2022).
12. Krakauer, Jon. *Under the Banner of Heaven: A Story of Violent Faith*. New York: Doubleday, 2003.
13. Krakauer, Jon. *Missoula: Rape and the Justic System in a College Town*. New York: Doubleday, 2015.
14. From opening monologue by Ricky Gervais at the 2020 Golden Globes ceremony. Abbey White, "Golden Globes: Read Ricky Gervais' Scathing Opening Monologue," *The Hollywood Reporter*, January 5, 2020, https://www.hollywoodreporter.com/news/general-news/transcript-ricky-gervais-golden-globes-2020-opening-monologue-1266516/.

Chapter 5

1. Kahneman, Daniel. *Thinking, Fast and Slow*. New York: Macmillan, 2011.
2. World Health Organization. "Chernobyl: The True Scale of the Accident."

September 5, 2005, https://www.who.int/news/item/05-09-2005-chernobyl-the-true-scale-of-the-accident.

3. "How Many People Died When the Titanic Sank?" *Encyclopedia Britannica*, n.d, https://www.britannica.com/question/How-many-people-died-when-the-Titanic-sank.

4. "Cause and Consequences of the Columbia Disaster." *Space Safety Magazine*, May 6, 2014, https://www.spacesafetymagazine.com/space-disasters/columbia-disaster/columbia-tragedy-repeated/#The%20Aftermath.

5. "BP Oil Spill | Environmental Damages, Claims & Settlements." Weitz & Luxenberg, April 13, 2021, https://www.weitzlux.com/environmental-pollution/gulf-oil-spill/.

6. Kahneman, *Thinking, Fast and Slow*.

7. Robbins, Tony. *Money: Master the Game: 7 Simple Steps to Financial Freedom*. New York: Simon and Schuster, 2014.

8. McRaven, Admiral William H. *Make Your Bed: Little Things That Can Change Your Life . . . and Maybe the World*. London: Hachette UK, 2017.

9. Ministerie van Algemene Zaken. "Prostitution." Government of the Netherlands, November 22, 2017, https://www.government.nl/topics/prostitution.

10. Dooling, Kathleen, and Michael M. Rachlis. "Vancouver's Supervised Injection Facility Challenges Canada's Drug Laws." *Canadian Medical Association Journal* 182 (13): 1440–1444, https://doi.org/10.1503/cmaj.100032.

Chapter 6

1. Backman, Fredrik. *My Grandmother Asked Me to Tell You She's Sorry*. New York: Simon and Schuster, 2015.

2. Connelly, Brian L., S. Trevis Certo, R. Duane Ireland, and Christopher R. Reutzel. "Signaling Theory: A Review and Assessment." *Journal of Management* 37, no. 1 (2011): 39–67.

3. Thaler, Richard H. *Misbehaving: The Making of Behavioral Economics*. New York: W.W. Norton & Company, 2015.

4. Connelly, Certo, Ireland, and Reutzel, "Signaling Theory," 39–67.

5. Goffman, Erving. *Frame Analysis: An Essay on the Organization of Experience*. Cambridge, MA: Harvard University Press, 1974.

6. Thaler, *Misbehaving*.

7. Gamble, Rupert, and Christensen. "Can Tax Policy Choice Architecture Motivate Positive Climate Change Actions?"

8. Levitt, Steven D., and Stephen J. Dubner. *Freakonomics: A Rogue Economist Explores the Hidden Side of Everything*. New York: William Morrow, 2009.

9. Voss, Christopher, and Tahl Raz. *Never Split the Difference: Negotiating as if Your Life Depended on It*. New York: Random House, 2016.

Chapter 7

1. "Demeter Biodynamic Certification." *Demeter USA*, n.d., https://www.demeter-usa.org/certification/.
2. Fox, Kenneth, Edward N. Gamble, and Pablo Muñoz. "The Non-Counting of Biodiversity for Sustainable Outcomes." Working paper, 2023.
3. "David Blaine: Quotes." IMDb, 2024, https://www.imdb.com/name/nm0086145/quotes/.
4. Garrahan, Matthew. "Lunch with the FT: John Lasseter." *Financial Times*, January 16, 2009, https://www.ft.com/content/d65cc760-e35a-11dd-a5cf-0000779fd2ac.
5. Weick, Karl E. "Small Wins: Redefining the Scale of Social Problems." *American Psychologist* 39, no. 1 (1984): 40.
6. Amabile, Teresa, and Steve Kramer. "Small Wins and Feeling Good." *Harvard Business Review* (2011).
7. Adriano, Andreas. "Poverty Fighters." *Finance & Development*, June 2020, https://www.imf.org/en/Publications/fandd/issues/2020/06/MIT-poverty-fighters-abhijit-banerjee-and-esther-duflo.
8. Grameen Foundation. "Breaking the Cycle. 2013–2014 Annual Report," 2014, http://www.grameenfoundation.org/sites/default/files/Grameen_Foundation_2014_Annual-Report_web.pdf.
9. Gamble, Edward N. "'Bang for Buck' in Microfinance: Wellbeing Mentorship or Business Education?" *Journal of Business Venturing Insights* 9 (2018): 137–144.
10. Al-Jazari, Isma'il Ibn al-Razzaz. *The Book of Knowledge of Ingenious Mechanical Devices*. Translated by Donald R. Hill. Boston: D. Reidel Publishing, 1974.

Chapter 8

1. *Star Wars Episode V: The Empire Strikes Back*. Beverly Hills, CA, Twentieth Century Fox Home Entertainment, 2004.
2. Morehead, James. "Stanford University's Carol Dweck on the Growth Mindset and Education." OneDublin.org, April 18, 2016, https://onedublin.org/2012/06/19/stanford-universitys-carol-dweck-on-the-growth-mindset-and-education/.
3. Yeager, David S. "Growth Mindset Study Shows Striking Effects for a Small Investment." The Holdsworth Center, October 24, 2019, https://holdsworthcenter.org/blog/growth-mindset-study-shows-striking-effects-for-a-small-investment/?gclid=Cj0KCQjwk7ugBhDIARIsAGuvgPbpOysgdxyM91CuqIfNrD40DXRGwhta8gpYXJ4_CPS7eUnzMAMsKV8aAn4TEALw_wcB.

4. Dean, Ben. "Defining Love of Learning." *Authentic Happiness*. Accessed March 15, 2024, https://www.authentichappiness.sas.upenn.edu/newsletters/authentichappinesscoaching/learning.
5. Nowik, Oskar. "14 Powerful Habits of People Dedicated to Lifelong Learning." *LifeHack*, August 18, 2023, https://www.lifehack.org/articles/communication/12-signs-you-are-lifelong-learner.html.
6. Gamble, Edward N. and Gary Caton. "Crafting Accountability: Unraveling the Micro-Foundations of Responsiblity." Working paper, 2024.

Chapter 9

1. Richard Branson (@richardbranson), "Opportunities are like buses—there's always another one coming!" X (formerly Twitter), November 1, 2012, 2:13 p.m., https://twitter.com/richardbranson/status/264067714266587136?lang=en.
2. Diamandis, Peter. "Peter's Laws: The Creed of the Persistent and Passionate Mind," 2023, https://www.diamandis.com/peters-laws.
3. Shane, Scott, and Sankaran Venkataraman. "The Promise of Entrepreneurship as a Field of Research." *Academy of Management Review* 25, no. 1 (2000): 217–226.
4. Shane, Scott A. *A General Theory of Entrepreneurship: The Individual-Opportunity Nexus*. Cheltenham: Edward Elgar Publishing, 2003.
5. Sarasvathy, Saras D. "Causation and Effectuation: Toward a Theoretical Shift from Economic Inevitability to Entrepreneurial Contingency." *Academy of Management Review* 26, no. 2 (2001): 243–263, https://doi.org/10.2307/259121.
6. Sarasvathy, "Causation and Effectuation," 243–263.
7. Bell, Alexander Graham. Alexander Graham Bell Museum, Baddeck, Nova Scotia, Canada.

Conclusion

1. Tsering's Fund. http://www.tseringsfund.org/.
2. Gamble, Edward N., Pablo Muñoz, and Kenneth A. Fox. "Is It Time to Clean Up US Tax-Exempt Nonprofit Reporting?" *Sustainability Accounting, Management and Policy Journal* 14, no. 1 (2022): 1–20.
3. Gamble, Edward N. and Srinivas Venugopal, "Is It Time to Rethink a Rich Man's View of a Poor Man's Needs? Impact Measurement through Recipient's Eyes." Working paper, 2024.
4. Muñoz, Pablo, and Edward N. Gamble. "When Given Two Choices, Take Both! Social Impact Assessment in Social Entrepreneurship." *Entrepreneurship and Regional Development*, Forthcoming 2024.

About the Author

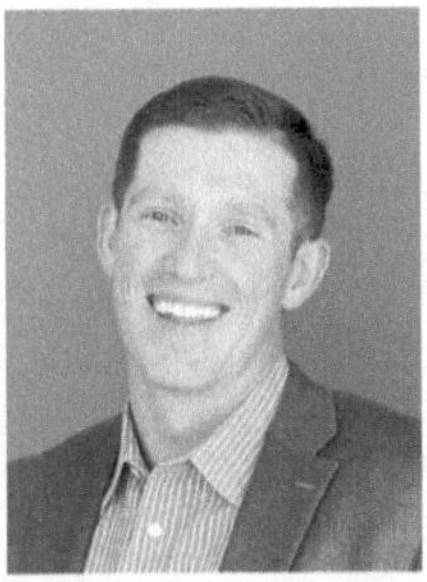

Amanda Stelling Photography

EDWARD GAMBLE has been an accounting and tax professor in the US for more than a decade. Currently he works at the University of Vermont, but he has also been a faculty member at Montana State University and a research fellow at the Initiative for Regulation and Applied Economic Analysis. Edward's PhD is from Lancaster University Management School (England), his MBA is from University College Dublin (Ireland), his Masters of Taxation is from Villanova University Law School (USA), and his undergraduate degree is from McMaster University (Canada). Edward is also a Chartered Professional Accountant (Canada).

Dr. Gamble's research examines accountability to improve venturing practices. This includes research in the areas of performance measurement, internal controls, social and environmental audits, fraud, social impact measurement, and tax policy.

Edward immigrated to Canada as a child from Ireland. He is a Canadian, Irish, and US citizen. To date he has worked and traveled extensively around the world in the regions of Asia, Africa, Australia, Europe, South America, Central America, and North America.

For more information on Edward, please feel free to visit www.edwardgamble.com.

www.ingramcontent.com/pod-product-compliance
Lightning Source LLC
Chambersburg PA
CBHW030443090526
44586CB00044B/597